Discerning
the Mystery

Discerning the Mystery

An Essay on the Nature of Theology

ANDREW LOUTH

CLARENDON PRESS · OXFORD

Oxford University Press, Walton Street, Oxford OX2 6DP

Oxford New York Toronto
Delhi Bombay Calcutta Madras Karachi
Petaling Jaya Singapore Hong Kong Tokyo
Nairobi Dar es Salaam Cape Town
Melbourne Auckland

and associated companies in
Berlin Ibadan

Oxford is a trade mark of Oxford University Press

Published in the United States
by Oxford University Press, New York

First published 1983
Reprinted 1985
First issued as a Clarendon Paperback 1989

British Library Cataloguing in Publication Data

Louth, Andrew
Discerning the mystery.
1. Theology
I. Title
201'.1 BR118
ISBN 0–19–826196–9 (Pbk.)

Printed in Great Britain by
Biddles Ltd, Guildford & King's Lynn

For
Evan Pilkington

Preface

THE seed of this book was two lectures on 'Theology and Spirituality' given to the Vacation Term of Biblical Studies at Oxford in the summer of 1979; that it germinated is due to the encouragement of Peter Spicer and Audrey Bayley of the Oxford University Press. Chapter V is based on a paper called 'In Defence of Allegory' given to the Oxford Society of Historical Theology in the spring of 1981. I am grateful to those responsible for inviting me on both occasions for the stimulus they provided, and to those who listened and helped with encouragement and criticism. Several people have helped by reading and commenting at various stages in the work, especially Robert Morgan, David Brown, and James Barr; pupils, colleagues, and even chance acquaintances have had some of the ideas presented here inflicted on them from time to time: to them all I am grateful for their response and their queries. Three people in particular have read a draft of the whole work and improved it enormously by their criticism and comments—John Barton, Sister Edmée SLG, and my wife—to them I owe a very great debt of gratitude. Naturally I am alone responsible for the use I have made of the ideas I have culled from others: I hope they will not feel I have adulterated them too much.

Feast of St Thomas the Apostle (Old Style)
1981

ANDREW LOUTH

Contents

Introduction

THIS work, as the subtitle indicates, is an essay, that is to say, it is not a definitive statement, but rather a suggestion intended to provoke not so much assent as discussion. It is written out of a consciousness of division in modern theology, and beyond that in the life of the Church. But such division is something that characterizes our culture as a whole and so the book starts from the sense of division and fragmentation found there. After a brief sketch of why we are where we are (or why we might be where we are), there is an attempt to focus on one of the ways in which the split in our culture manifests itself. It seems to me that the most striking, and alarming, aspect of this split is in the one-sided way we have come to seek and recognize truth, a one-sidedness which can be traced immediately, though doubtless it has deeper roots still, to the Enlightenment and the belief that the sciences fulfil the promise the Enlightenment held out to mankind. This one-sidedness is manifest in the way in which all concern with truth has been relinquished to the sciences, and to those branches of learning that can successfully adopt the methods of the sciences. In the humanities this has partly involved the development of the so-called social sciences, and partly the development within the traditional disciplines themselves of the historical-critical method, as a kind of analogue to the scientific method. Along with this there is a kind of fatalism: conscious that other men were men of their time, we are conscious of the way we belong to our time and feel constrained to think in certain ways. As Leslie Houlden said, in his contribution to *The Myth of God Incarnate,* 'we must accept our lot, bequeathed to us by the Enlightenment, and make the most of it'.[1]

The approach of this book, after setting the scene, is to examine first just what this 'lot bequeathed to us by the Enlightenment' amounts to. Although the claim of the scientific method to be the paradigm of any search for truth has been widely conceded, we find that from the time of the eighteenth-century Italian Vico onwards there has been resistance to this claim, a resistance

[1] Ed. John Hick (London, 1977), p. 125.

that has carved out for the humanities a role as an intellectual endeavour, alongside of, but different in its procedures from, the sciences. In chapter II we look at Vico, the first to make such a claim, and Dilthey, the most brilliant to explore it. With Dilthey we find a striking attempt to describe the way of proceeding in the humanities that has been enormously influential, even though his influence has often passed unnoticed in the English-speaking world, as Dilthey has not been at all well known here. In particular his influence has been great and acknowledged in Germany, and the influence of German theology on Anglo-Saxon theology, especially in the realm of biblical studies, needs no comment. But for all the brilliance of Dilthey's attempt to justify the humanities as intellectual disciplines with their own methods, it seems in the end that Dilthey concedes to the sciences the concern with objective truth, leaving to the humanities only a concern with the way we make sense of our experience as human beings. It is then that we turn to the thought of the Heidelberg philosopher Hans-Georg Gadamer, who was a student of both Bultmann and Heidegger at Marburg, which is a sustained—and to me convincing—attack on the fundamental claim of the Enlightenment that science is the way to truth and the only way to truth. In his great work, *Truth and Method,* Gadamer puts forward an analysis of the legitimacy of (in his own words) 'an experience of truth that transcends the sphere of the control of the scientific method':[2] an experience of *truth*, be it noted; Gadamer is not prepared to concede all concern with truth to the sciences. This is a more radical—and more promising—way of resisting the totalitarian claims of science than we find in Vico and Dilthey, to whom of course Gadamer owes a great deal. In effect, Gadamer sees science as *one* way of apprehending truth, not *the* way, and he thus situates science within a total approach to truth, rather than seeking to tailor the ways of apprehending the truth to the methods of the sciences.

And yet theology has traditionally been thought of as a science, indeed as the queen of the sciences, and so in chapter III we look at the most significant attempt in recent years to rethink the notion of theology as a science and thus elucidate the question of theological method, found in the works of T. F. Torrance.

---

[2] London, 1975, p. xii.

It seems to me, however, that it is in Gadamer's recovery of the humanities' own proper engagement with truth that we can find a closer analogy to the ways of theology. But first, by way of the reflections of the nineteenth-century theologian F. J. A. Hort, and the twentieth-century scientist and philosopher Michael Polanyi, on the nature of scientific investigation, I suggest that in reality science as a human pursuit of truth is much less privileged that the claims of the Enlightenment might lead us to suppose. Polanyi sees scientific ways of knowing as dependent upon tradition and the 'tacit dimension' (as he calls it), and from a perspective very different from Gadamer's brings forward a strikingly similar critique of the presuppositions of the Enlightenment. More is involved, though, than a mere critique, for there is an impressive unity about the pattern underlying any of the human apprehensions of truth discerned by both Gadamer and Polanyi. And it is a pattern that ought to be familiar to the theologian, for, as I shall argue, it is the pattern underlying the thought of the Fathers of the Church. By means of a distinction between problem and mystery, drawn from the reflections of Gabriel Marcel, this point is given greater focus and its implications for epistemology explored.

The rest of the book seeks to explore this pattern and see if there is anything here that will help us to gain greater clarity and sense of purpose in the theological task. First, consideration is given to the notion of tradition, which has an important role in Patristic theology. Then attention is focused on the Fathers' use of *allegory* in the interpretation of Scripture, for, as we shall see, this is part of the tradition, both in the obvious sense that it is a traditional way of interpreting Scripture, and in a deeper sense, in that allegory draws on the notion of tradition, plays on it (as it were) in such a way as to draw out the hidden depths of the tradition. But I also concentrate on allegory for another reason: because it is the Fathers' use of allegory which, more than anything else, renders their theology suspect, and even frankly incredible, to those who have imbibed the presuppositions of the Enlightenment, presuppositions which I have argued to be increasingly incredible and naîve themselves in the light of the critique of such as Polanyi and Gadamer.

A final chapter seeks to draw all this together and point to the unity of theology by means of the idea of 'living the mystery', the idea that theology is not just perception of, but response to, the mystery of God in Christ.

Throughout the work there is frequent citation of other writers. This is partly in the nature of a running acknowledgement of the debt I owe to those who have inspired my own reflections, but it also serves the important purpose—so it seems to me—of indicating that the theological scene is much more varied and exciting than sometimes appears to be the case.

I. DISSOCIATION OF SENSIBILITY

A consciousness of division, a yawning gulf, that penetrates into our very heart and mind, a failure, an inability to relate: much of this is characteristic of modern culture and society. It has been described and analysed in different ways, and generally deplored, though usually helplessly. With this sense of division goes a sense, often enough, that things have not always been like this—that they need not be like this. But this sense of division, too, is felt to be alarming, fateful, in its implications:

> Things fall apart, the centre cannot hold;
> Mere anarchy is loosed upon the world,
> The blood-dimmed tide is loosed, and everywhere
> The ceremony of innocence is drowned;
> The best lack all conviction, while the worst
> Are full of passionate intensity.

The very familiarity of these lines of Yeats is telling. We look back and try to discern the lost unity: when and how it was. T. S. Eliot spoke of a 'dissociation of sensibility' that set in in the seventeenth century and from which we have never recovered: a dissociation manifested in the way in which the refinement of language in the eighteenth century is not matched by any corresponding refinement of feeling—rather the reverse. It is a dissociation between thought and feeling, between the mind and the heart. Romanticism is acutely conscious of this division and gropes after the lost unity: Wordsworth's language of the 'feeling intellect' is an example. But, as a phenomenon, Romanticism is rather an example of such dissociation of sensibility, rather than the beginnings of a cure. Much that happened in the nineteenth century in the wake of Romanticism built on this dissociation of sensibility and deepened it, rather than administering any kind of cure. The whole development in the nineteenth century of art as a kind of specialization—or a group of specializations—can be seen in this light. We have the music of the virtuoso, the art of the genius: the net effect of this is to alienate art from any real context in life. Beauty, instead of being something we might find in life, and something that has to do with life, is relegated to the fringes of life: and consequently is only of concern to those who have the leisure to spend much time at the fringes. (The very self-consciousness of the efforts of Ruskin and others to prevent this, only bears out the truth of such an analysis). We find art for art's sake: art as the potentiality for pure aesthetic experiences, and the cultivation of an aesthetic consciousness by those who have the time and inclination to indulge. Such a marginalization of the aesthetic is simply an attempt to live with this dissociation of sensibility, an attempt to regard it as normal.

Theology does not escape all this, indeed it is even possible for theologians to present religion as one of the aesthetic possibilities open to a cultured minority. The very subtitle of Schleiermacher's famous *Speeches on Religion*—'to the cultured among its despisers'—shows that such was his apologetic strategy. But the case with theology is in some respects different: the crack and divisions go deeper and have been there longer, and it might even be argued that it is the collapse of the centre in theology that has led to the spreading of the cracks throughout our culture. In any case, it is certain that much of the division in theology is simply a reflection of the division in our culture: the specialization in theology, the remoteness of theologians—often complained of—from the Church and the believing Christian, and indeed the remoteness of theologians from one another (the Old Testament specialist from the specialist in nineteenth-century theology, say) are all part of a phenomenon we see much of elsewhere and have come to regard as inevitable. One way in which the division in theology manifests itself is in the division between theology and spirituality, the division between thought about God and the movement of the heart towards God. It is a division of mind and heart, recalling Eliot's 'dissociation of sensibility', and a division which is particularly damaging in theology, for it threatens in a fundamental way the whole fabric of theology in both its spiritual and intellectual aspects. Cut off from the movement of the heart towards God, theology finds itself in a void—for where is its object? Where is the God with whom it concerns itself? Even if God can be reached by reason, even if natural theology is possible, real theology could never be confined within

such narrow limits. For theology (as opposed to religious
studies) concerns itself with the Scriptures, with tradition, with
the development of dogma, with the history of the Church, all of
which is natural enough to the Christian, to one who *believes*. But
belief, faith, is not a purely rational exercise; it involves, as an indispensable element, the response of the will or the heart to the
One in whom we believe. Cut off from this, theology has to
justify itself, not directly, but indirectly, as an indispensable part
of historic European culture, for example. It is an uneasy justification, and inevitably pushes theology to the periphery, to be
studied not for itself, but for some usefulness that can be claimed
for it.

And such a division undermines Christian prayer too; for
Christian prayer is the movement of the heart *towards God*,
towards a God who has revealed himself in Jesus Christ. Prayer
is not simply the movement of the heart, but is the response of the
heart to God's love manifest in Jesus Christ. Cut off from
theology, prayer loses its objectivity, its concern with reality. For
Christian prayer cannot be confined, as perhaps other forms of
prayer can, to some spiritual or mental activity—meditative or
contemplative—which is of value in itself and needs no further
justification. Prayer is engagement with the object of our faith,
an object which is in some way apprehended or known; and in
such cognitive engagement the *mind* is involved. Faith is, to use
the traditional phrase, *cum assensione cogitare*, to *think* with assent.
We do not just feel something in prayer, we know something.

The proposition that the division between theology and spirituality is linked with the division in our culture is confirmed by
the language of the Greek Fathers, for there we find both terms
naturally translated by the same word, *theologia*. For the Fathers
theologia is both wider and narrower than our term, 'theology'.
It is narrower in that it is strictly discourse about *God*: in the
Cappadocian Fathers it means the doctrine of the Trinity, God
as He is in Himself, in contrast to *oikonomia*, the doctrine of
God's dealings with his creation; though it can be used to include
that. It cannot, however, be used in the way we use 'theology'
when we speak of, for example, a 'theology of society'. At the
same time, *theologia* for the Fathers is broader than our term, for
it means not just the *doctrine* of the Trinity, but *contemplation* of
the Trinity. *Theologia*, for Evagrius, a friend and disciple of the

Cappadocians, is precisely contemplation, *theoria*, of God, as opposed to contemplation of the cosmos. A theologian for him is one who has attained this state of pure prayer: 'if you are a theologian, you pray truly, and if you pray truly, you are a theologian'.[1] There is here no division between theology and spirituality, no dissociation between the mind which knows God and the heart which loves him. It is not just that theology and spirituality, though different, are held together; rather *theologia* is the apprehension of God by a man restored to the image and likeness of God, and within this apprehension there can be discerned two sides (though there is something artificial about such discrimination): what *we* call the intellectual and the affective. Naturally these two aspects *are* present, and one or the other can predominate: St. Basil's *Liturgy* is prayer, his book *On the Holy Spirit* is theology, though the latter is not without passages of prayerful ecstasy, and in the former the mind is concerned to express something with exactness and clarity; but the two aspects are not to be separated.

But whatever is the case with the Fathers, for us there is an almost unconscious division between theology and spirituality; even if we feel they belong together, we have to relate them to each other, and not all theologians want to relate them too closely. The commitment that prayer implies seems to some to compromise the 'objectivity' of theology as a rational study. The centre does not hold: the object of theology retreats, and is displaced. Theologians become more concerned with one another, and less with the God who is the traditional object of their study. Kierkegaard's impression of the state of theology remains appropriate: 'To me the theological world is like the road along the coast on a Sunday afternoon during the races—they storm past one another, shouting and yelling, and when at last they arrive, covered with dust and out of breath—they look at each other and go home.'[2]

When and how this division entered theology is a question on which many different views are held. Some point to the way the Fathers themselves accuse the heretics of such a division, to the

---

[1] *Treatise on Prayer* (ascribed, traditionally, to St. Nilus), c. 61 (in the enumeration of the chapters in the *Philokalia*, Venice, 1792).

[2] *The Journals of Søren Kierkegaard*, ed. and trans. by A. Dru (London, 1938), entry 16 (p. 9).

accusations levelled at such as Arius and Apollinaris, for example, of being merely logicians and in that way severing theology from its real concern with God in prayer. From such a perspective, the division in theology is simply evidence of a growing faithlessnesss in theology: theology as it has been in the West, the complaint usually goes on, has declined further and further from its pristine condition. Those who make such a charge usually stand aside, in some way, from the cultural development of the West: they see themselves as representing a remnant faithful to the original faith of the Church. It is characteristic of some theologians of the Eastern Orthodox Church, for instance. Others see the original unity breaking up at some point in the cultural development of the West. This breakup is not necessarily seen as a bad thing. In the twelfth century there emerged an institutionalized divergence between the universities, which had grown out of the Cathedral schools, and the monasteries: the conflict between St. Bernard and Abelard is seen as symbolic. It is a fairly widely held view (associated in England, especially perhaps, with the name of Beryl Smalley) that it is in the Cathedral schools that we see the beginnings of the modern study of the Bible, which eschews the allegorizing of the Fathers and the Dark Ages. According to this view, study of the Bible is freed from the suffocating nets of allegorizing tradition and becomes an intellectually respectable subject. The breakup of the original unity is seen as a release. But that is not an unquestionable interpretation of the events, nor one that commends itself to the approach of this book: we can see in the writings of the twelfth century—on both sides of the growing divide—a separation between mind and heart that had not been the case with the Fathers. With Augustine (to take an example from the West, since we are concerned with later developments in the West) knowledge and love are held together: there is a co-inherence of love and knowledge—we cannot love what we do not know, nor do we progress in knowledge if we do not love—which is characteristic of the movement of Augustine's thought. With Bernard, however, this is no longer the case: knowledge and love are juxtaposed, and love is more fundamental.[3] Augustine's rejection of *curiositas,* for him the rejection of a

---

[3] See my article in *The Influence of St. Bernard,* ed. Sister Benedicta Ward SLG (Oxford, 1976), pp. 1-10.

distracting obsession with knowing things, takes on in St. Bernard an anti-intellectualist slant. Here, though there may be
some sort of advance,it is at the expense of wholeness.

But it is also fairly common—and makes a good deal of
sense—to see the original unity of the Patristic vision not collaps-
ing with the rise of scholasticism, but finding there its final
flowering. St. Thomas Aquinas and St. Bonaventure, in different ways, can be seen to bear witness to this. Such is the view
of Henri de Lubac, whose ideas I shall discuss later. For such a
view the divide comes after St. Thomas, in later medieval
scholasticism beginning with Scotus and Ockham. The use of
the so-called 'doctrine of the two powers of God', that is, the
systematic distinction between what God *could* have done absolutely (*potentia absoluta*) and what he has in fact ordained (*potentia ordinata*), opened up the possibility of a great deal of purely
theoretical discussion, and certainly contributed to the barren-
ness of later medieval theology (often called 'nominalist'). It is
not by chance that the fourteenth century sees the rise of this
kind of theology and also the rise of an affective mysticism that is
often frankly mistrustful of academic theology. The attitude of
Thomas à Kempis, who belongs to this tradition of affective
mysticism, towards academic theology is well known.

It is important to be aware of such theories about the development of medieval theology, for it certainly prepared the way for
what is our more immediate concern: the currents of thought
that have shaped the world in which we live, by which I mean,
primarily, the Renaissance, the rise of modern science, and the
Enlightenment. The extent to which the roots of the Renaissance
and the rise of modern science reach back into the Middle Ages,
to the 'renaissance' of the twelfth century, and to such figures as
Grosseteste and Roger Bacon, is variously estimated, but none
of it sprang like Minerva from the head of Jove, fully formed.
What is important for an understanding of the condition of
modern theology, though, is an awareness of how much it owes
to these currents of thought and their culmination in the
Enlightenment. For since then the mainstream of theology has
been swept along by the currents of the day, and has, in a fairly
direct way, reflected contemporary cultural preoccupations.

The Renaissance is often represented as a break with tradition
(though someone like Erasmus thought that he was discovering

the true tradition which had been obscured by the later Middle Ages), for the discoveries made during those years of intense enquiry led to the undermining of late medieval society and the particular symbiosis of Church and society that characterized it. The rediscovery of the classics revealed a world quite different from that of late medieval times, and men were startled to find that their society was not inevitably the only way society could be. Particular discoveries, like the discovery that the document called the *Donation of Constantine,* which purported to be Constantine's gift of lands to the papacy, was a forgery, undermined in a more precise way the pretensions of the late medieval Church. Erasmus' text of the Greek New Testament, with his own translation of it into Latin, likewise revealed that the text of Scripture traditionally used in the Church was not the only possible one, nor even the best possible. The traditional way of understanding things—something inherited—was shaken. How then was man to know the truth? Clearly he had in some way to find it out for himself.

It is here, it seems to me, that the characteristic emphasis of what we still think of as modern emerges: an emphasis which is to underlie the confidence of the Enlightenment, and which, for reasons that will emerge, survived the collapse of *that* particular confidence. It is the idea that there is a *method* by which we can reach the truth, 'a general method through which, it was held, any kind of subject-matter must be approached, if knowledge of that subject was to be attained'.[4] The delineation of this method by such as Descartes and Locke was the first step towards a universal science, a *mathesis universalis.* It is less important for us to grasp how Descartes and Locke understood this method than to realize the significance of their having discovered a method. Knowledge, truth, was now open to man: all he had to do, in any area of knowledge, was to apply the method. Man starts in ignorance and confusion, but by application of the method is led towards light and truth. Doubt, an attempt to free oneself from prejudice and preconception, an attempt to reduce the subject-matter to simple items which could be discerned clearly and distinctly, is then followed by a piecing-together of the simple items into a body of reliable knowledge (two processes Schouls

---

[4] A. Schouls, *The Imposition of Method* (Oxford, 1980), p. 5.

calls, in the book from which we have already quoted, 'resolution' and 'composition'). Such an approach to knowledge involves a break with tradition, not only in the sense that it is a different way of proceeding from what preceded it, but also in a more fundamental sense: for it destroys the notion of tradition altogether. According to Descartes, and even more Locke, man's mind is a *tabula rasa* upon which ideas are to be freshly written; there are no 'innate understandings'. The word 'prejudice' acquires pejorative overtones: it means simply an unfounded judgement, which is therefore to be rejected. A statement is not conceded to be true simply because it is correct, but only if it can be shown to have a proper methodological justification.

What is important, however, is not the detail of the method itself, but the idea that there is a method which will lead one to the truth, and perhaps even more important still, the fact that the application of this method has led to astounding results in the realm of the natural sciences. The argument from success is very difficult to resist, and advances in science since the seventeenth century have been nothing if not successful. In this realm the insight of Descartes and Locke has been proved up to the hilt: the scientific method is a way of getting at the truth, and a way that succeeds. But the scientific method is perhaps easier to characterize than the method Descartes and Locke were investigating (indeed it is rather different from what Descartes envisaged). It is an experimental method, that is, it involves the use of experiments in order to test hypotheses. Gradually a science, a body of tested knowledge, develops; later scientists take for granted the results of their predecessors, unless they have serious reason to doubt them. Experiments are *repeatable,* and it is crucial that they should be repeatable by other experimenters. In this way the individuality of the experimenter is eliminated, and we arrive at *objective* truth, truth that is not subjective, that does not depend on the one who is perceiving it. And because experiments must be repeatable, they must concern themselves with that which can be repeated, that is, that which can be quantitatively characterized or measured. So we have a scientific method which is experimental, concerned with that which can be quantitatively characterized or measured, and which leads to a truth which is the same for all. All this is certainly over-simplified: hypotheses are not to be understood in the isolated way my brief account has suggested, they grow out of a model that is heuristic—a way of proceeding (by trial and error)—rather than descriptive, and make little sense outside that model; nor is the notion of the repeatability of experiments that methodologically excludes the experimenter quite as simple as it looks—Heisenberg's 'uncertainty principle' qualifies all this, though it is not clear that it is any more than a qualification. Some aspects of all this will be raised again in chapter III.

We have, none the less, the spectacle of the scientific method as a proved way of attaining truth. One crucial element in it is that it is concerned with what can be quantitatively characterized, and it is here that mathematics enters to provide a means of handling such quantitative characterization. It is indeed through mathematics that the objectivity of the truth attained by science is to be grasped, and though in theory this could possibly be reduced to verbal expressions (though it is not clear that it can), for all practical purposes it is only in mathematical form that the truth of much of modern science is expressible. It has been suggested (by George Steiner[5]) that this has led to a fundamental division within our human understanding between two languages in which truth can be expressed: the language of mathematics and the language of words. And it is the former, the non-verbal, language which has been able to prove itself as the grammar, as it were, of the scientific method. It is the language of mathematics that can grasp and express truth, and not our ordinary language of words. Here we come across another fundamental dissociation between a silent truth and a verbal something else. Steiner gives an example from his own experience of having 'watched topologists, knowing no syllable of each other's language, working effectively together at a blackboard in the silent speech common to their craft'.[6]

We thought we had a method which would lead us to the truth and we have discovered that the scientific method is indeed such a method—one which has been immensely successful. It is, moreover, a method which ultimately prescinds from our usual form of discourse, verbal language, and uses the non-verbal

---

[5] In his article 'The Retreat from the Word', in *Language and Silence* (Harmondsworth, 1969), pp. 31-56.
[6] Ibid., p. 34.

language of mathematics. Perhaps, we think, we have here the
way forward. In the article, 'The Retreat from the Word', from
which we have already quoted, Steiner has suggested that this is
indeed the temptation which has beset the humanities in the last
few centuries:

> There has taken place in history, economics and what are called,
> significantly, the 'social sciences', what one might term a fallacy of im-
> itative form. In each of these fields, the mode of discourse still relies
> almost completely on word-language. But historians, economists and
> social scientists have tried to graft on to the verbal matrix some of the
> proceedings of mathematical or total rigour. Many have grown defen-
> sive about the essential provisional and aesthetic character of their own
> pursuits ... The ambitions of scientific rigour and prophecy have
> seduced much historical writing from its veritable nature, which is art.
> Much of what passes for history at present is scarcely literate. The
> disciples of Namier (not he himself) consign Gibbon, Macaulay or
> Michelet to the limbo of *belles lettres*.[7]

The term *belles lettres* is, of course, highly significant, witnessing
to the marginalization of the aesthetic we have already mentioned; for such writing is merely aesthetic, merely elegant, not to be
taken seriously, not concerned with what is true. Recently in his
valedictory lecture as Regius Professor of History at Oxford,
Hugh Trevor-Roper protested against the attempt to reduce
history to an objective science and defended its status as one of
the 'arts': 'Objective science has its place in historical study, but
it is a subordinate place: the heart of the subject is not in the
method but in the motor, not in the technique but in the
historian.'[8] The article of Steiner's is, in fact, an analysis of the
way humane culture has lost its nerve since the seventeenth century, lost its confidence in the word, grown accustomed to a
fragmentation that contains gulfs of incomprehension, and now
seems to face the prospect of a return to chaos. And a symptom of
this is the 'fallacy of imitative form' whereby humane culture
relinquishes to a scientific method, dependent upon the non-
verbal, non-humane language of mathematics, concern for what
is true.

But the 'fallacy of imitative form' manifests itself not only in
the illiteracy of much that passes for what used to be humane

[7] Ibid., pp. 37-8.
[8] *Times Literary Supplement* (25 July 1980), p. 833.

culture. It is part of the story of the development of the humanities since the Enlightenment at a deeper level. The 'method' which will lead us to truth has been more difficult to come by in the humanities than in the sciences, and if come by at all, it has certainly not been nearly as successful. And yet, like a mirage or will-o'-the-wisp, it has beckoned men on. Where is the method for the humanities that will lead us to truth? What is the analogue for the humanities to the scientific method? Again what is important is rather the determination to find a method than the precise form the method takes. And as we look at the way such a method was discovered, we shall find that what is important are the presuppositions that underlie the search.

Although the scientific method, because of its manifest success, seems to provide a paradigm for the method by which, in any area of knowledge, we are to seek the truth, if we wish to find a parallel method for the humanities, there are a number of obvious problems. The humanities are all historical, in the sense that they do not study what is independent of any particular time, as is the case with the sciences, but study man in society, his language, his thought, and actions. And though it is possible to abstract man from his circumstances, this is much less possible than the corresponding abstraction in the sciences. It is difficult to conduct experiments; indeed it is strictly speaking impossible, though it is possible to regard history as a vast laboratory in which experiments are always taking place. (Something like this is presumably true, *mutatis mutandis,* of astronomy: experiments are not conducted but deemed to be taking place—so that problems arise over rare, or even in principle unrepeatable, events, the beginnings of the universe, for example.) Descartes, and others of his contemporaries, did not regard history as a genuine realm of knowledge at all: it was gossip, hearsay. A scepticism was engendered that threatened to cut man off from his past altogether.

But a method might seem to emerge for the humanities if this fact—that the humanities are concerned with what men have done in history, what men have done in the past—is taken as the key to the problem. For the writings of the past reveal a world which is different from ours, they show us a past which is remote from us. And much of the remoteness strikes us as simply incredible. One way of proceeding, one way of attempting to establish truth about the past, is to use our experience of the present as a criterion for assessing statements about the past. What is congruent with our experience is to be accepted, what is incongruent is to be rejected as incredible. This was Voltaire's way, guided by what he called *le bon sens*. But to us it looks a rather rough-and-ready way of proceeding, whatever its value at the time. As Isaiah Berlin says, '*Le bon sens* served Voltaire well: it enabled him to discredit much clerical propaganda and a good many naive and pedantic assertions ... on the other hand, he found no difficulty at all in accepting the reality of satyrs, fauns, the Minotaur, Zeus, Theseus, Hercules, or the journey of Bacchus to India ...'.[9]

If *le bon sens* is the beginnings of a method of reaching truth from the writings of the past, with Spinoza we find something altogether more subtle. The credible (judged so according to the canons of our own experience) is accepted, but the incredible is not, as with Voltaire, simply discarded. Instead we are to say to ourselves, 'What must men who thought as they did have meant by writing this, which is to us incredible?' Spinoza called for an act of imaginative conjecture whereby we try to see the world through the eyes of these ancients who describe a world that seems so strange to us. But it is only when the world they describe is incredible that we need have recourse to such an imaginative leap: the credible can be understood as if they were our contemporaries. So, for example, Euclid is to be read and understood in a straightforward manner, whereas the miraculous stories of the biblical narrative demand of us an imaginative leap. Such a method of explaining away the miraculous (for that is what it amounts to) was a much more effective way of attacking Christianity than simply discounting miracles as incredible.

But we can take this a step further. The method of understanding the writings of the past by thinking oneself back into the minds of the ancient writers need not be restricted to passages in their writings which seem incredible: it can be applied generally. And this was indeed the position of the Romantics. In rejecting the rationalism of the Enlightenment and its confident sense that

---

[9] *Against the Current* (London, 1980), p. 91.

mankind had now reached a level of rationality that placed him above the dark ages of the past, the Romantics sought to see all ages as equally important, equally immediate to God; they looked to the past with enthusiasm and sympathy. Gone was the superior discrimination between 'credible' and 'incredible' in the tradition: all was to be understood 'historically', all was to be understood by an imaginative leap into the minds of the ancient writers. But the ambivalence of this approach was overlooked: for, however great its enthusiasm for the past and its sympathy with the writers of the past, such an approach treats them all as if they were false. Whereas the Enlightenment discriminated and used a rudimentary method of historical understanding on that part of the tradition it deemed to be false, the Romantics, in effect, treated the whole of the tradition as false. 'Historical consciousness' (as we call this approach of the Romantics and their successors), while trying to establish a link with tradition that had been weakened by the Enlightenment, in fact finally broke that link altogether.

But we now have a method for exploring historical reality— the method of 'historical consciousness' or the 'historical-critical method'—and, with this method we can again hope to find the humanities established as branches of knowledge, as sciences. That this is what we are about in employing this method, that we are seeking respectability *vis-à-vis* the sciences, comes out in the sort of language used of this method. Its practitioners speak of a 'scientific' approach to texts, of the 'scientific' study of the past, and although the word 'scientific' can simply mean having to do with knowledge (*scientia*), it has in English a more restricted denotation, as 'science' and 'the sciences' now refer paradigmatically to the natural sciences, the 'exact' sciences, and to call something scientific is to evoke this paradigm. (This is less so in German and French where *Wissenschaft* and *science* are not as restricted in their significance.) To call a branch of study 'scientific' is to claim that it has found a way of applying the methodology of the sciences: and it is the use of the historical-critical method that gives colour to this claim in the humanities.

But now an utterly horrendous division opens up within the humanities themselves. The historical-critical method enables

us to study the history of philosophy, for example: we are enabled to look at the philosophers of the past and place them in their
historical context. Their philosophical views are seen to be a
reflection of their historical situation, which can be analysed in a
number of different ways. One can look at the great sweep of the
history of philosophy and see the earlier philosophers con-
tributing to some great enterprise of the progress of the human
spirit. Hegel is perhaps the first, and most brilliant, example of
such an approach to philosophy, and he finds his successors in
such as Windelband and Zeller. One can also take the line that
what really engenders progress, the movement from one age to
another throughout history, is not what men think at all, but
something deeper. Marxism takes such a line: the real deter-
minants of history are economic, the history of ideas is a reflection of this. The sweep we find in the history of ideas does not
have its coherence in itself, it is the reflection of economic reality,
where development really takes place. But either way, whether
the history of philosophy presents itself to us as a coherent subject or not, the philosophers are no longer of interest in
themselves; they are interesting only as they contribute to the
history of the subject. A gulf opens between history of philosophy
and philosophy itself: philosophers need have no interest in the
history of their subject and historians of philosophy certainly
need not be philosophers. This division between the humanities
and the history of the humanities has very curious effects. It is of
course parallel to the divide between science and the history of
science: the history of science is not a science, is not pursued by
scientists; it is in fact one of the humanities, a branch of history.
But it is a natural divide; for scientists study nature, whereas the
history of science studies man: scientists and their thought and
ways of procedure. On the other hand, a division between any
one of the humanities and its history has no such rationale.
Philosophers do not just think in isolation—though Descartes
claimed to have thought out most of his philosophy all by himself
(while meditating all day in a stove)—they discuss with one
another, read one another: and most of the philosophers worth
reading are dead. This history of philosophy contains much of
the material for their thought. One recalls in this context T. S.
Eliot's remark: 'Someone said: "The dead writers are remote

from us because we *know* so much more than they did''. Precisely, and they are that which we know.'[10]

The consequences of this divide between the humanities and their history can take two sharply different forms. If the practitioners of (let us say) philosophy are fairly confident about their subject, then the past literature of the subject becomes a quarry for philosophical argument, and the development of the subject is seen as progress towards the present state of the subject, which is now at its highest stage of development. The history of the subject is interesting as the tracing of progressive enlightenment: as we look back we see the errors from which man has been delivered by the advance of knowledge. One does not look to the past to learn anything from it, though the various elements in what we know now can be seen to have developed in the past; and often enough the great philosophers of the past who first thoroughly explored some element or another of what is now regarded as assured knowledge are worth careful study, for in them we find a classic treatment of what we know now. They are 'still' relevant, we say: a way of putting it that suggests that one day they will be superseded.

That is when there is some confidence in the subject. When that confidence is lacking, the picture looks rather different: then we are aware rather of the fact that we are just about to pass into history, just about to form part of the flow of the subject through history. Conscious that what we have learnt from an objective study of the history of our subject is that even the great figures of the past are carried along by influences and strands of historical development of which they were perhaps quite unconscious, we fall back in our own study of the subject into a fatalistic subjectivism. This can easily be illustrated from modern theology, which is deeply affected by a crisis of confidence.

So, for instance, the late Professor Lampe had this to say in the report *Christian Believing*:

No one can entirely extricate himself from the complex tradition to which he belongs. He cannot clear the ground and build a new system of belief, using the primary data of revelation as its sole foundation. The believer's exploration into truth cannot set out into uncharted territory. It consists not so much in pioneering as in attempting to

[10] *Selected Essays* (London, 3rd edn. 1951), p. 16.

analyse, criticize and evaluate a set of beliefs and attitudes towards belief, which he has derived from a long stream of tradition, and, where they seem inadequate or misleading as expressions of the faith to which he finds himself committed, to restate, modify or replace them.[11]

It is not so much what is said here with which I would want to take issue, as the attitude it betrays. Professor Lampe speaks of the faith 'to which he finds himself committed' and thus betrays the fatalism which underlies his attitude: he does not so much believe as find himself believing. And this fatalism is only the rebound from a striving-after a historical objectivity which eludes him: the believer cannot 'entirely extricate himself from the complex tradition to which he belongs'. With confidence in the subject, that would not matter: what matters, then, is not how the human spirit progresses but that it does (Arthur Koestler's account of the history of the Copernican revolution in *The Sleepwalkers* does not undermine the scientist's confidence that this was indeed a decisive step forward). But if there is a crisis of confidence, the strands of tradition seem like shackles that bind us and condemn us to a subjectivism from which we helplessly long to escape. Thus trapped, the believer cannot 'clear the ground and build a new system of belief'.

Now, this crisis of confidence which affects theology is entirely justified if theology continues on the path that has been laid down by the Enlightenment and the Romantics. For it is a path which leads theology away from the heart of the subject, and *is meant to*. The historical-critical method is a way of explaining away what does not fit within a fairly narrowly defined, rationalistic enterprise. As we have seen, it was first used to explain away miracles. Generalized by the Romantics, it explains away the past altogether. Nothing like traditional Christianity can survive in such an environment, for such traditional Christianity claims that through certain specific events in the past God has revealed himself to men. As Dom Gregory Dix well put it, 'It is not myth or allegory which is at the heart of [the mystery of the Christian Faith] but something rooted in a solid temporal event, wrought out grimly and murderously in one Man's flesh and blood on a few particular square yards of hillock outside a gate, *epi Pontiou Pilatou*'[12] If the past is rendered inaccessible, Christianity will have to change pretty radically in order to survive.

[11] London, 1976, p. 100.
[12] *The Shape of the Liturgy* (Westminster, 1945), p. 748.

II. THE LEGACY OF THE ENLIGHTENMENT

THE idea that there is a fundamental difference between the sciences and the arts (or humanities) is relatively easy to indicate in general terms. In the sciences we find a clear notion of progress: textbooks go out of date, the advances of the past are incorporated into the whole body of science and studied in that context; the great scientists of earlier times are not directly studied by the modern student of the sciences. None of this is true for the arts. If there is progress, it is much more equivocal and it is difficult to reach agreement as to its nature. What progress has there been since Homer, or Sophocles, or Plato? This question cannot be answered in the same way as we would answer the question, 'What progress has there been since Archimedes, or Hippocrates, or Newton?' None the less, from the beginnings of the modern period, as we have seen, some, impressed by the advance of science, have tended to think that the difference between the sciences and the arts is to the disadvantage of the latter; they have called into question the intellectual seriousness of the arts. Lack of progress has been regarded as a *failure,* and attempts have been made to remedy this state of affairs by finding some way whereby the arts can attain a like success to the sciences. On the other hand, there has been a whole current of reflection, also part of the legacy of the Enlightenment, that has seen a real difference between the sciences and the humanities, and has resisted any tendency to assimilate the latter to the former: it is this current of reflection we shall explore in the present chapter.

In his article 'The Divorce between the Sciences and the Humanities',[1] Sir Isaiah Berlin sees the consciousness of a radical difference between the sciences and the arts emerging as a protest against the tendency of the Enlightenment to regard the advances of modern science as proving the paradigmatic character of the sciences for all human knowing. The first

---

[1] *Against the Current* (London, 1980), pp. 80-110.

person, Belin tells us, in whom this protest was apparent was the Neapolitan writer, Giambattista Vico (1688-1744). Vico's first step in questioning the Enlightenment ideal of progress towards clear, objective knowledge of the world around us was his interpretation of the place of mathematics in scientific thinking. Mathematics seems to be a discipline which leads to wholly clear, irrefutable propositions of universal validity. This is, according to Vico, an illusion. Mathematics is not a discovery, but a human invention. It deals with axioms and definitions, devised by men, which lead to conclusions that logically follow because the procedures involved, likewise devised by men, see that they do. Mathematics is wholly transparent, leading to clear, definite results because the whole thing is a game, devised by men and played by men: it is 'a play of abstractions controlled by their creators'. Once this system is applied to something outside men's minds—let us say in physics or mechanics—it yields important truths, in so far as it can be made to apply, but since nature is not man's invention, there is not a perfect 'fit' between mathematics and the reality to which it is being applied, there is not the absolute clarity and certainty that we find in mathematics itself. Indeed, the 'exactness' of science is a function of the extent to which nature can be tailored to fit mathematical axioms: in physics it is relatively easy, in biology it is more difficult, so physics appears to be a more 'exact' science than biology.

Vico brings into play here a scholastic tag at least as old as St. Augustine: that one can only fully know what one has oneself made. With mathematics there is complete knowledge since it is entirely a human creation. But with nature, God's creation, complete knowledge is denied to us because we have not made it: only God can wholly know nature. Nature remains always opaque to us; we cannot know it from inside, we cannot understand it; that is only possible for what we have created.

But Vico made the crucial step when he realized that human history is something man has made, and which he can therefore know from within. He saw that human history, to quote Berlin, 'did not consist merely of things and events and their consequences and sequences (including those of human organisms viewed as natural objects) as the external world did; it was the story of human activities, of what men did and thought and suf-

fered, of what they strove for, aimed at, rejected, conceived, im-
agined, of what their feelings were directed at. It was concerned,
therefore, with motives, purposes, hopes, fears, loves and
hatreds, jealousies, ambitions, outlooks and visions of reality;
with the ways of seeing, and ways of acting and creating, of individuals and groups. These activities we knew directly, because
we were involved in them as actors, not spectators. There was a
sense, therefore, in which we knew more about ourselves than
we knew about the external world ...'.[2] The realm of human
history is more immediate to us than the natural world: it is
therefore more possible for us to understand it than the natural
world. And it therefore displays a peculiar perversity, thought
Vico, to seek to use the methods with which we explore the
natural world, which is opaque to us, in order to understand the
realm of human history, which is in some sense transparent to us.

But how do we understand the realm of human history?
Vico's approach has a number of elements. One is an appreciation of metaphor and the indispensable role it plays in our
attempt to represent to ourselves reality. Metaphors are not
simply embellishments of what could equally easily be stated in
plain, literal prose. Metaphors, rather, disclose a way of looking
at the world, a way of understanding the world. If we wish to
understand the way in which any of the ancients understood
their world, we must pay heed to their use of metaphors, we must
enter into their metaphorical view of the world. It is a strange
world we shall find revealed to us and it will not be easy for us to
enter it. It will, Vico insisted, require enormous effort, but it will
be quite a different sort of effort from that demanded of the scientist who seeks to devise experiments which will prise from nature
her secrets: it will be an effort not of exact, logical, deductive
thought, but of sympathy and *imagination*.

It is imagination, *fantasia*, that is at the heart of Vico's attempt
to enter into the realm of human history. What is involved is an
imaginative reconstruction of, an entering into, the world of past
societies, of past cultures. Societies, and cultures: for Vico had
a profound sense of the way in which men are shaped by the
society in which they live. The metaphors, which reveal to us
the world of thought of the ancients, are not to be seen as the

---

[2] Ibid., p. 95.

ingenious conceits of individuals, but as reflections of the common sense (the *sensus communis*) of that society. Indeed this notion of *sensus communis* is fundamental to Vico and (as Ernesto Grassi had argued[3]) is closely bound up with his notion of *fantasia*. The *sensus communis* is prior to the reflective intelligence, and forms the basic preconceptions of a culture or society. As Vico puts it, 'The human will, highly unstable as it is by nature, is rendered firm and definite by the *sense common* to all men with respect to what is needed by and useful to them: these are the two sources of the natural law of nations. The sense that is common to all is a judgement without reflection, universally felt by an entire group, an entire people, a whole nation or the whole of the human race.'[4]

Such an enterprise is clearly very different from the ways suggested by the scientific method. Vico, indeed, suggests that it is not only very different, but more natural and more accessible to us than the enterprise of the natural scientists:

in the night of thick darkness enveloping the earliest antiquity, so remote from ourselves, there shines the eternal and never failing light of a truth beyond all question: that the world of civil society has certainly been made by men, and that its principles are therefore to be found within the modifications of the human mind. Whoever reflects on this cannot but marvel that the philosophers should have bent all their energies to the study of the world of nature, which, since God made it, He alone knows; and that they should have neglected the study of the world of nations, or civil world, which, since men had made it, men could come to know.[5]

With Vico, suggests Berlin, a gap has 'opened between natural science and the humanities as the result of a new attitude to the human past'. 'Vico began this schism,' Berlin goes on to say: 'after that there was a parting of the ways. The specific and unique versus the repetitive and the universal, the concrete versus the abstract, perpetual movement versus rest, the inner versus the outer, quality versus quantity, culture-bound versus

---

[3] In 'The Priority of Common Sense and Imagination', in *Vico and Contemporary Thought* (ed. G. Tagliacozzo, M. Mooney, D. P. Verene: London, 1980), pp. 163-85.

[4] *La Scienza Nuova*, bk I, sect. II, paras. 11-12 (ed. P. Rossi, Milan, 1977: pp. 178-9), quoted in his own trans. by Grassi (n. 3), p. 170 (in the standard English trans., *The New Science of Giambattista Vico* (rev. trans. of 3rd edn. by T. G. Bergin and M. H. Frisch, New York, 1968), paras. 141-2).

[5] Ibid., bk I, sect. III (Rossi, pp. 231-2; Bergin and Frisch, para. 331); quoted by Berlin (n. 1), p. 106.

timeless principles, mental strife and self-transformation as a permanent condition of man versus the possibility (and desirability) of peace, order, final harmony and the satisfaction of all rational human wishes—these are some of the aspects of the contrast.'[6]

It is very much this kind of divide between the sciences and the humanities that informs the approach of Wilhelm Dilthey (1833-1911), who reflected deeply on the question and whose reflections have been enormously influential throughout this century. His starting-point was the failure of attempts to transfer the methodology of the empirical sciences to the humanities. The reason for this failure lay, in his view, in the different kinds of evidence available in the two areas of the natural sciences and the humanities: the natural sciences are concerned with physical objects which can be described and measured and analysed with great precision, the humanities are concerned with human minds which are not accessible to us in that way. On the other hand, human minds are accessible to us in a more fundamental sense: for, while we cannot enter into the being of physical things and processes, we can enter into the nature of human beings and societies with a kind of sympathetic insight, because there is a common identity of nature, human nature, between us and them. In the sciences we study what is alien to us—physical things; in the humanities what we study is connatural with us. Dilthey does not use this difference in any way to depreciate the natural sciences: he is interested rather in how it enables us to understand the different methodologies appropriate to the humanities (*Geisteswissenschaften,* as he called them, sciences of the (human) spirit, in contrast to *Naturwissenschaften,* the natural sciences).

How do we understand minds, he asked? Even with our own minds, we do not simply understand ourselves by a process of reflexive introspection. We understand our experiences through trying to express them to ourselves, through trying to grasp them in what Dilthey calls 'expressions'. In the case of other minds we come to understanding through interpreting their expressions. Through the common nature all minds share, we can enter into the mind of another through its expressions, through the way it

---

[6] Berlin, p. 109.

expresses itself—through a sympathetic understanding of its expressions. As Hodges puts it in his study of Dilthey, 'I see a human figure in a downcast attitude, the face marked with tears; these are expressions of grief, and I cannot normally perceive them without feeling in myself a reverberation of the grief which they express. Though native to another mind than mine, and forming part of a mental history which is not mine, it none the less comes alive in me, or sets up an image or reproduction of itself (*Nachbild*) in my consciousness. Upon this foundation all my understanding of the other person is built.'[7] This process is not one of inference: that is, I do not deduce from the other's expression that he is grieving; it is an immediate, emotional, not intellectual, response that is awakened in me by the sight of someone in grief. Such understanding is very close to sympathy: though sympathy is something else—what happens when, seeing someone in grief, I not only understand that he is grieving, but feel pity for him and, as it were, grieve with him.

This capacity to relive the experience of another is what gives one access to the minds of others. This process is, however, usually much more complex than a simple mental reproduction of the experience understood, just as it happened. In a conversation one's capacity to enter into the mind of the other is fed by one's understanding of the grammatical structure of his sentences, and the logical structure of his thought, as well as by a sensibility to what is not said and an awareness of his gestures, tone of voice, and so on. A similar complexity is found if one seeks to understand the behaviour of someone over a period of time, or seeks to understand a play or a novel. This complexity involves considerable intellectual effort, an effort of analysis and sifting, attempting to fill in gaps and work out a coherent and plausible account. In this intellectual activity we are guided, according to Dilthey, by the principle of coherence: a true interpretation of whatever it is we are asking to understand will be one which is coherent with itself and consistent with what we know of human nature. The way in which this principle of coherence acts as a guiding light is something that Dilthey regards as characteristic of the humanities, and it is one of the

[7] H. A. Hodges, *Wilhelm Dilthey: An Introduction* (London, 1944), p. 14. This book contains a lucid discussion of the thought of Dilthey, and a short selection of passages in translation from his works.

points of contrast between the natural sciences and the humanities to which he likes to draw attention. As Hodges put it, 'Our knowledge of the physical world comes from disjointed sense-data which come to us with no objective unity or coherence in them, and a minimum of order in the shape of causal sequence has to be imparted to them by the perceiving mind itself, as Kant made clear; but in the mind we see the principle of unity, it is given in inner experience and projected in understanding, and in working with this principle we are not imposing an interpretation on the phenomena, but tracing their own inherent structure.'[8]

Interpretation, then, involves, a great deal of assembling of evidence and reasoning in an ordinary logical way, but this is not the heart of the process: the heart of the process is the simple ability to reflect in the mind the experiences of another, an ability which is realized in what Dilthey calls the process of 'indwelling'. Interpretation is, fundamentally, what Hodges calls 'a process of imaginative amplification' of this fundamental capacity; it is the process of indwelling whereby one seeks to enter into another's experience. What makes interpretation possible at all is the capacity man has, in virtue of being a self-conscious mind, to enter into the minds of others.

It is this that lies behind Dilthey's hermeneutics, his science (as it were) of interpretation. The aim in interpretating any literary work is to enter into the mind of the writer. The method involves both linguistic and historical skills: one must know both the language and the historical context of the writer one is seeking to understand. But here emerges a circle—the so-called 'hermeneutical circle'—which is characteristic of this sort of interpretation at every level. We must understand the historical context of a work in order to understand it: but the work itself is evidence for the historical context in the light of which it is to be understood. And most of the other evidence for the historical context of any particular work are other works, which themselves need to be interpreted before they can yield any evidence of the historical context. The same is true of language: one learns a language by seeing how it is used, from examples of its use. And the same is true, in another way, of any particular

[8] Ibid., p. 17.

literary work: only when we understand the whole can we understand its parts, and only as we understand its parts can we
understand the whole. This is the 'hermeneutic circle' which
we must enter in order to understand, and yet can only enter by
understanding. 'This circle is logically unbreakable, but we
break it in practice every time we understand.'[9] We begin with a
rough view of the whole and in the light of this, attempt to
understand the parts; in the light of the understanding thus
gained we revise our understanding of the whole, and then move
back to an understanding of the parts. This to-and-fro movement between the parts and the whole proceeds until we have an
interpretation, coherent in itself, which does violence to none of
its parts, and fits the historical circumstances as known to us.
Thus we attain understanding. But this process is not a purely
logical process, or even primarily a logical process, for it is a
process of *understanding*, a way of entering into the mind of the
author, which is achieved by what Dilthey, like Schleiermacher,
calls an element of 'divination'. A good interpreter 'feels his
way' into the mind of his author by a kind of insight which is fre-
quently incapable of proof, and often he sees things in a work of
art of which the author himself was not conscious—in Schleiermacher's phrase, often repeated by Dilthey, 'he understands the
author better than he understood himself'.

Vico and Dilthey, then, develop similar points of contrast between the natural sciences and the humanities. Both emphasize
the way in which our understanding of nature, though objective,
is external, in contrast to the understanding possible to us in the
humanities, an understanding from 'inside' based on the connaturality of all human minds. The method of science is logical
and rational; the method of the humanities is one of imagination,
sympathetic understanding, 'indwelling'. But as presented by
Vico and Dilthey the contrast between science and the humanities still seems to concede to the Enlightenment that truth is
something discovered by means of science and the scientific
method: what they are claiming for the humanities is not exactly
that they uncover truth, but that they are worth while. This
comes out very clearly in Isaiah Berlin's interpretation of Vico.
The 'unaltering character of basic human nature' is, he says,

9 Ibid., p. 27.

shattered by Vico: the cultures of the past are different from ours and different from one another. These cultures are opaque to one another: truths in one culture are not truths in another; humanly perceived reality is culture-bound. If this is really what Vico means, one wonders what has become of 'the eternal and never failing light of a truth beyond all question: that the world of civil society has certainly been made by men, and that its principles are therefore to be found within the modifications of the human mind': what could be meant by that if all human truths are culture-bound? In drawing attention to the immense variety of human understanding of the world, Vico certainly rules out any *simpliste* attempt to hold them all together; and his system of *corsi e recorsi* does suggest mutually incompatible states of civil society. But the contradictions and puzzles of Vico's writings are manifold.[10]

A similar problem arises for Dilthey in his doctrine of *Weltanschauungen,* the three fundamental ways of interpreting the world, or three fundamental attitudes to the world, none of which can be regarded as ultimate or absolute.[11] These three *Weltanschauungen* he called *naturalism, the idealism of freedom,* and *objective idealism.* The first, naturalism, is that view of things based on the animal side of man's nature which revolts against any kind of other-worldliness: it is this world that attracts its attention, and man is seen as at home in this world. The idealism of freedom is based on the experience of free will and moral obligation: it sees the key of meaning in the notion of personality. Objective idealism is based on the experience of the self as a whole and it sees in the universe a wholeness and living unity like that of the self. Although Dilthey himself felt greatest temperamental affinity for the last *Weltanschauung,* he recognized that each world-view (and the manifold compromises between them that are possible) has its own claim to validity. It is not easy to see how such a view can ultimately avoid the suggestion of an abandonment of truth in favour of some form of cultural relativism. And the same problem presents itself in the case of Collingwood, the Oxford philosopher, influenced by Dilthey, whose ideas we shall look at later. His doctrine of metaphysics as

---

[10] See Berlin (n. 1), p. 115.
[11] See Hodges (n. 7), pp. 99-108.

the history of absolute presuppositions seems to lead to a kind of
cultural relativism in much the same way as Dilthey's doctrine of
Weltanschauungen.[12] A similar kind of relativism is often held to be
involved in Dilthey's doctrine of the hermeneutical circle, which
is taken by some as proof that truth is unattainable in the
humanities, rather than as a description of the way in which
understanding is achieved in the humanities. Hodges himself
provokes the same kind of unease. In his Gifford Lectures,
published as *God beyond Knowledge,*[13] where he is clearly indebted
to Dilthey though no longer speaking as his interpreter, Hodges
makes a basic distinction between knowledge, which is concerned with truth and which is advanced by the scientific method,
and life-paradigms, which depend on commitment and are not,
strictly speaking, matters of truth or falsity at all. In the light of
this distinction, theology, or a theistic faith, is clearly, for
Hodges, one of the life-paradigms, and so not concerned with
truth at all. In the light of such a position, any attempt to
assimilate theology (which in any traditional sense is concerned
with truth) to the sciences, however different its methods of
study are from those of scientists, is understandable, though, as I
shall argue in the next chapter, mistaken.

Is it the case, though, that the attempt to understand the
humanities as radically different from the sciences inevitably involves acquiescence in 'culture-bound' truths, which hardly
seem to be truths at all, and the opting for a subjectivism which
concedes to the sciences any real concern for ultimate truth?

The kind of distinction between the sciences and the arts that
we have been discussing in this chapter is a distinction which
has been articulated in the context of the growth of *historical
consciousness* over the last couple of centuries. It is our sense of
historical consciousness that brings out the peculiar nature of
the humanities and their distinction from the sciences. The
sciences are ahistorical; they deal with a natural order that has
always been much the same as it is. The humanities are historical; they deal with the doings of men who are shaped by the
historical contexts in which they live. But while the awareness
of historical consciousness brings with it an awareness of the

[12] See ibid., p. 102, for a comparison of Collingwood and Dilthey.
[13] London, 1979.

peculiar nature of the humanities as forms of knowledge, it may also contain unexamined presuppositions that qualify the nature of this insight. And we may begin to suspect this when we see an awareness of history—historical consciousness—smuggling in as a method, parallel to the scientific method, a way of procedure calling itself the historical-critical method. For such a method may unconsciously bring with it presuppositions that underlie the scientific method but which are not appropriate to the humanities. There do in fact seem to be a number of inter-related presuppositions being thus introduced. One is the notion of objective and subjective truth, and another, it will be argued, is a privileged position being ascribed to the present, or what is thought to be the present.

Science is concerned with objective truth, that is, with truth inhering in the object of knowledge. Such truth is independent of whoever observes it, and it is precisely this that the use of the experimental method seeks to achieve. As we have seen, the experimental method seeks to elide the experimenter by the principle that experiments must be repeatable by other experimenters. Objective truth, in this sense, seeks to be detached from the subjectivity of the observer. In contrast to such objective truth, subjective truth is a truth which cannot be detached from the observer and his situation: it is a truth which is true for me, and which cannot be expressed in such a way that it is true for everyone. Put like that, it seems at first sight obvious that objective truth is real truth, and subjective truth falls short of such ultimacy. But further reflection suggests that so to suppose is to over-simplify. When Kierkegaard claimed that all truth lay in subjectivity, he meant that truth which could be expressed objectively (so that it was the same for everyone) was mere information that concerned everyone and no one. Real truth, truth that a man would lay down his life for, was essentially subjective: a truth passionately apprehended by the subject. To say, then, that truth is subjective is to say that its significance lies in the subject's engagement with it; it does not mean that it is not objective in any sense: indeed if it were objective in no sense, if it were simply a collection of subjective impressions, there would be no engagement, and consequently no question of truth at all. If, then, we concede that the humanities are concerned with subjective truth, as opposed to the objective truth sought by the sciences, this need not imply that they are concerned with what need not be true, what is not absolute, but it does imply (and this is the most important sense of subjective truth) that the humanities are not primarily concerned with establishing objective information (though this is important), but with bringing men into engagement with what is true. What is important is engagement with reality, not simply the discerning of reality: and if it *is* reality, then it has a certain objectivity, it cannot be simply a reflection of my subjective apprehensions.

We must be careful, then, not to try and introduce into the humanities a false ideal of objectivity derived from the sciences; and yet, we shall suggest, it is just this that the historical-critical method seeks to do. But this striving after objectivity has another odd leaning in that it tends to lead to a kind of canonization of the present. We have already seen something of what this means when we looked at Voltaire's use of the principle of *le bon sens*: Voltaire's 'good sense' canonizes what he finds credible, what he is used to—the past is measured against the present. That this is part of a general tendency can be seen if we try and think through what is involved in an attempt to incorporate scientific ideas of objectivity into the humanities. We can see this if we reflect that in a way the roles of space and time are divided between the sciences and the humanities: the sciences are concerned with what is independent of history, for them space is the primary dimension, and the concern for objectivity can be seen as an attempt to eliminate errors due to perspective, the perspective of the individual observer. In the humanities, which are concerned with what men have thought and felt and done, time is the primary dimension: here objectivity is going to mean an attempt to overcome the effect of time's flow, an attempt to achieve immediacy with the past. It is, then, the pastness of the past that presents problems to our understanding: it is the past that is the problem. But the past in contrast to what? Not the literally present, the *now*: for the present is fleeting, we cannot possess it or arrest its progress. It is then the *recent* past against which we are measuring the more remote past. The recent past is thought to be comprehensible and acts as a criterion for the more remote past. There is little logic in it, and yet this is the consequence of trying to elide the subjectivity of the present, which contains the one who seeks to understand, in an attempt to achieve an objectivity about the past thought to be possible if it does not contain the subjectivity of the one seeking to understand.

But even the idea that the past, because it is *past,* poses problems for the understanding, suggests the corollary that understanding the present poses no problems, which is hardly likely. Even in a conversation between two people with similar backgrounds, words do not simply convey a meaning that the other unequivocally decodes. We each use words with our own private echoes, based on our own history; what we say is capable of several interpretations and it is only as a result of engagement with another in conversation that we attain any mutual understanding—*engagement,* in this context an attempt to fit my words to what I perceive to be another's preconceptions and expectations, and an attempt to discern these by imaginative listening. *Total* understanding of another is impossible, even in the present, because the intended meaning may slip, for a variety of reasons, through the net of expression and interpretation.[14] Understanding and interpretation is a problematic undertaking in itself. The past may pose its own problems—and does—but they are not the only problems of understanding there are; and most of the problems of the past are those we meet in any attempt to communicate and understand.

One of the most interesting attempts to reflect on the distinctive approach of the humanities, an attempt which examines critically the notion of 'historical consciousness' and the historical-critical method that offers itself within this context, is the work of Hans-Georg Gadamer, *Truth and Method.*[15] This is a considerable work and represents a profound and far-reaching attempt to reorient the humanities. It is, professedly, an attempt to show 'how little the traditions in which we stand are weakened by modern historical consciousness': it is, then, an attempt to recall the humanities to their true nature. Gadamer sees the humanities affected by what Steiner has called the 'fallacy of imitative form' in their attempt to reproduce the methodology of the sciences by use of the historical-critical method. What

---

[14] On this see G. Steiner's reflections in *After Babel* (London, 1975), especially the first chapter.

[15] *Wahrheit und Methode* (Tübingen, 4th edn. 1975). English translation: *Truth and Method* (London, 1975, from the 2nd German edn), which I have used in my citations (with occasional modifications).

follows will be a discussion very much guided by Gadamer's ideas, though there can be no attempt here to reproduce the ramifications of his thought, for they build up a whole picture with a coherence that will hardly be disclosed by our more straitened discussion.

The historical-critical method is, on the analogy of the scientific method, a way of reaching objective truth, that is, truth that inheres in the object, independently of the one who knows this truth. It is necessary, then, to locate the objectivity that it is the purpose of the method to reach. This is done by ascribing to the object of study, which in the humanities focuses on the writings of men, a 'meaning' which is there independently of any understanding of it, an objective meaning which the historical-critical method attempts to discover. With Dilthey, and the Romantic tradition of interpretation, to which such ideas belong, the meaning is not so much the meaning of the literary text itself, as the meaning which lies behind the text and which becomes accessible to us as we enter into the mind of the author, divine his meaning, and 'understand him better than he understood himself'. The method is the reconstruction of the original historical context, as we have already seen. But all this presupposes that the subjectivity of the one who is seeking to understand can be elided—and not surprisingly, for that is what the experimental method *is* seeking to achieve in the sciences. Such an elision is much less convincing in the humanities, precisely because of the connaturality that exists between the author and his interpreter which is lacking in the sciences. Both the writer and I who seek to understand him belong in history: I cannot reconstruct his historical situation and think myself into it, as if I had no historical context myself. And even were such a thing possible, what would be achieved would be no more than a dead meaning, whereas meaning and understanding is something that takes place: takes place, that is, in the present. Understanding a past writer is, in Hegel's phrase, a 'thinking mediation with present life' (denkende Vermittlung mit dem gegenwärtigen Leben): it is an engagement with a past writer so that I hear his meaning in the present, my present. The meaning of an author is something that emerges in an engagement between the reader and an author: it cannot be limited by the subjectivity of the author, nor by the capacities of the 'original reader'—indeed, as Gadamer remarks, 'the idea of the original reader is full of unexamined idealization'.[16] Any writing, any creation of literature, is the creation of *tradition,* of what is handed on. 'What is fixed in writing has detached itself from the contingency of its origin and made itself free for new relationships. Normative concepts such as the author's meaning or the original reader's understanding represent in fact only an empty space that is filled from time to time in understanding.'[17] Gadamer indeed goes further in discussing the false objectivity ascribed to the original meaning of the author. As he points out, for Schleiermacher, Dilthey, and the Romantic tradition of interpretation in general, the object of understanding is not *what* the writer said, but the writer himself. It is the 'Thou' of the author we are trying to understand, and we seek to achieve this understanding by going behind what the author said. This means we do not understand a literary text in terms of its objective content, but as an 'aesthetic construct'. Against this, Gadamer would set a different notion of understanding, one, he would claim, that is truer. What the Romantics have in mind is not understanding in the sense of agreement between two people about something: when this happens I have understood someone in the sense that I have understood what he was saying. Rather they have in mind what they think of as a deeper understanding—not simply an understanding of what another has said, but an understanding of *him*: a getting-beneath the skin of another so that I understand not only what he has said, but also what he failed to say, whether through deception or imperfect self-knowledge—an understanding of which one could well say that 'I have understood him better than he has understood himself.' Against this, both for reasons of what is attainable, and for other deeper reasons which will emerge later, Gadamer sets the notion of understanding as agreement between two people about something, and thus sees in our understanding of an author an engagement with what he has said. This frees us from the false objectivity of the 'original meaning'. 'Not occasionally only, but always, the meaning of a text goes beyond its author': an author's meaning is found by engagement with his text, with what he has said. This does not

[16] Ibid., p. 356.
[17] Ibid., p. 357.

mean that, as in Romantic interpretation, our understanding of what has been written is superior to that of the writer himself: 'it is enough to say that we understand in a different way, if we understand at all'.[18]

More of what is involved in all this emerges if we look at the other side of this attempt in the humanities to emulate the scientific method. Corresponding to the false objectivity of the meaning of a literary text which is there and only needs to be elicited by application of the method, there is the attempt to overlook or elide the subjectivity of the one who is engaged in understanding. This comes out particularly clearly in the ideal of presuppositionless understanding, the ideal of freeing myself of presuppositions in order to understand the objective meaning of the text. It was noted in chapter I that the purely negative meaning which attaches to the word 'prejudice' is a legacy from the Enlightenment. A prejudice against prejudices is an attempt, which was the aim of the Enlightenment, to deprive tradition of its power. Freed from tradition and the prejudices that it bears, the individual can understand the past 'objectively'. 'But', Gadamer asks, 'does the fact that one is set within various traditions mean really and primarily that one is subject to prejudices and limited in one's freedom? Is not, rather, all human existence, even the freest, limited and qualified in various ways? If this is true, then the idea of an absolute reason is impossible for historical humanity...'.[19] Gadamer goes on to point out the *individualism* of the Romantic approach. For Dilthey it is pure experience (*Erlebnis*) that is primary, and in his attempt to understand the past Dilthey is particularly attentive to autobiography and similar achievements of introspection. The result of this is to make history 'private'. But is it not the case that the historical realities of society and the state have a predeterminate effect on any 'experience'? 'In fact,' as Gadamer puts it, 'history does not belong to us, we belong to it. Long before we understand ourselves through the process of self-examination, we understand ourselves in a self-evident way in the family, the society and the state in which we live. The focus of subjectivity is a distorting mirror. The self-awareness of the individual is only a flickering in the closed circuits of historical

[18] Ibid., p. 264.
[19] Ibid., p. 245.

life. That is why the prejudices of the individual, far more than his judgements, constitute the historical reality of his being.'[20]

The individualism of the Romantic theory of interpretation attempts to abstract the individual from his historical context by presenting him with the ideal of presuppositionless understanding; a truer theory of interpretation, which does not seek to elide the historical reality of the one seeking understanding, sets the interpreter himself within tradition. What we understand when we seek to understand the writings of the past is borne to us by tradition. Understanding is an engagement with tradition, not an attempt to escape from it. We have seen that the process of understanding in the humanities involves a circular movement of thought, the so-called 'hermeneutic circle'. For the Romantics the hermeneutic circle can be regarded as a provisional state, which ultimately vanishes in perfect understanding when we find ourselves in the mind of the author. But for a truer doctrine of interpretation the hermeneutic circle does not vanish in understanding: rather the circle *is* understanding. 'The circle, then,' says Gadamer, 'is not formal in nature, it is neither subjective nor objective, but describes understanding as the interplay of the movement of tradition and the movement of the interpreter. The anticipation of meaning that governs our understanding of a text is not an act of subjectivity, but proceeds from the communality that binds us to the tradition.'[21] The discovery of the true meaning of a text or of a work of art is never finished—there is no 'original meaning'—it is rather an infinite process whereby tradition is handed on.

Gadamer's attempt to avoid the false objectivity of the method of historical criticism involves an attempt to reinstate tradition and the authority of tradition. He argues that tradition is appropriate to the human reality we are seeking to engage with in the humanities. For in the humanities we are concerned not with the natural world of objects, but with the moral world of free persons. And this moral world is transparent to us in a way that the natural world is not (a point familiar to us from Vico). This

[20] Ibid.
[21] Ibid., p. 261.

transparency is reflected in the human achievement of language and literature:

> The mode of being of literature has something unique and incomparable about it ... There is nothing so strange and at the same time so demanding as the written word ... The written word and what partakes of it—literature—is the intelligibility of mind transferred to the most alien medium. Nothing is so purely the trace of mind as writing, but also nothing is so dependent on the understanding mind. In its deciphering and interpretation a miracle takes place: the transformation of something strange and dead into a total simultaneity and familiarity. This is like nothing else that has come down to us from the past ... a written tradition, when deciphered and read, is to such an extent pure mind that it speaks to us as if in the present. That is why the capacity to read, to understand what is written, is like a secret art, even a magic that looses and binds us. In it time and space seem to be suspended. The man who is able to read what has been handed down in writing testifies to and achieves the sheer presence of the past.[22]

Language and literature disclose to us the moral realm of free human agents: the *moral* realm, because we understand it by analogy with the way we understand ourselves. In it we are confronted with the mystery of human freedom, as opposed to the puzzle of the interaction of natural laws; and this is a mystery in which we participate. 'The world of history depends on freedom, and this remains an ultimately unplumbable mystery of the person. Only the study of one's own conscience can approach it, and only God can know the truth here. For this reason historical study will not seek knowledge of laws and cannot call on experiment. For the historian is separated from his object of study by the infinite intermediary of tradition.'[23] But this intermediary of tradition, although it does exclude experiment and the search for that sort of objectivity, is the bearer of positive meaning and truth: 'it is not a yawning abyss, but is filled with the continuity of custom and tradition, in the light of which all that is handed down presents itself to us'.[24] This 'continuity' is the continuity of human communication, an experience of the transparency laid bare by language and literature: '"hearsay" is here not bad evidence, but the only evidence possible'.[25] Understood like

[22] Ibid., p. 145.
[23] Ibid., p. 191.
[24] Ibid., pp. 264-5.
[25] Ibid., p. 191.

this, tradition is the context in which one can be free, it is not something that constrains us and prevents us from being free. 'The fact is that tradition is constantly an element of freedom and of history itself. Even the most genuine and solid tradition does not persist by nature because of the inertia of what once existed. It needs to be affirmed, embraced, cultivated ...'.[26] The act of interpretation is one of the ways in which tradition is 'affirmed, embraced, cultivated' and passed on.

From such a point of view the idea of an *antithesis* between tradition and reason, tradition and historical research, history and knowledge is rejected. Rather, tradition, as preservation, is an act of reason, and interpretation is engagement with what is presented to us by tradition. There is no longer any need to try and forget our preconceptions or prejudices when we seek to understand something written in the past (or indeed someone who lived in the past): 'all that is asked is that we remain open to the meaning of the other person or text ...'.[27] There is nothing new in this, but it runs across the grain of a Romantic doctrine of interpretation—Theodor Haecker bore witness to it when he wrote in *Vergil: Vater des Abendlandes:*

I am not talking about Vergil and Vergilianism without presuppositions. No one does that or can do it, whatever or whomever he speaks of. Each consideration or description is based on a principle, even if on the nihilistic principle of being without principles. Man acknowledges nothing without presuppositions, even nothingness itself presupposes fulness of being, not vice versa. It is not presuppositionlessness in general and in itself which is the requirement of an exact science, but on the contrary, the possession of the fulness of all presuppositions which belong to a determinate object both subjectively from the side of the one in pursuit of understanding and objectively on the side of the object. Certainly, for a *historian* as a rule the present is confusion and darkness, things must lie at a certain distance before they can have or reveal a meaning, but then also they have it within living history only through things which lie before us, which for better or for worse have indeed to be presupposed as *true things*. If then, for example, someone demands of me that I speak of Vergil and Vergilian man without presuppositions, then I will ask him what he means by that. Is he demanding of me that I should speak, in the words of the ancient

---

[26] Ibid., p. 250.
[27] Ibid., p. 238.

historian, *sine ira et studio,* that is without yielding to any disposition, without any passion that clouds the vision, without any egotistical or partial purpose? Good, he is doubtless right. Is he demanding of me not to permit what does not proceed from the object itself? Good, he is again right. But is he demanding of me that I should leave out in my analysis of Vergil and Vergilian man 'the' faith, the greatest concern of the West, the emergence, so close to Vergil, of Christendom, that I should determine it *only* from its past and what was immediately contemporary with it and not from its future, which now lies in the past and still lies in the present, then he asks of me what is improper and absurd.[28]

The last way in which Haecker makes his point in this passage corresponds very closely to one of the points Gadamer wishes to make. 'Historical consciousness' is conscious of history as something which affects the object of our historical study: to this Gadamer opposes what he calls *Wirkungsgeschichte* and *wirkungsgeschichtliches Bewusstsein* (translated as 'effective history' and 'effective historical consciousness'), by which he means not simply an awareness of the historical context of the object of our study, but an awareness of history as it bears on the present, and brings into the historical situation of the interpreter that which we are seeking to understand. So Haecker insists that we must be aware not just of the past and contemporary influences on Vergil, but also of Vergil's influence on the history, the tradition, that has made him accessible to us. And our situation is something in which we are inextricably bound up; we cannot jump out of our historical skins and gain objective knowledge of the situation in which we are. 'Clarification of this situation, that is, reflection on the bearing of history on ourselves is not capable of completeness, but this lack of completeness is not a defect of such reflection, rather it lies in the nature of historical being, which we are.'[29] The fact that we exist in history means that knowledge of ourselves can never be complete.

If we accept the implications of this—that interpretation of the past is not an attempt to transcend tradition, but rather an engagement with tradition; that the one who seeks to understand the past cannot himself step outside his own situation but is seeking an understanding of the past in the present, a present which

---

[28] Munich, 5th edn. 1947, pp. 16-17.
[29] *Truth and Method,* p. 285.

bears upon him in ways of which he cannot be objectively aware; that this engagement with the past is not simply a process whereby we understand the past, but equally a process of self-discovery which can never be complete—if we accept the implications of this, we can begin to see what is involved in any process of understanding within the humanities. It is a process of revising our preconceptions, not seeking to escape from them. It is a growing into what we learn from tradition. The movement in the process is a movement of *un*deception: as a result of experience and growing understanding we see that we have been deceived and so are freed from deception. It is thus a growth in truth, and a growth in openness towards new experiences. As Gadamer puts it, 'the truth of experience always contains an orientation towards new experiences. The perfection of this experience, the perfect form of what we call "experienced", does not consist in the fact that someone already knows everything and knows better than anyone else. Rather the experienced person proves to be, on the contrary, someone who is radically undogmatic; who, because of the many experiences he has had and the knowledge he has drawn from them is particularly well equipped to have new experiences and to learn from them. The dialectic of experience has its own fulfilment not in definitive knowledge, but in that openness to experience which is encouraged by experience itself.'[30] This growth in experience is not primarily an increase in knowledge of this or that situation, but rather an escape from what had deceived us and held us captive. It is learning by suffering, suffering the process of undeception, which is usually painful.

Learning by suffering—*pathei mathos,* in Aeschylus' phrase; but this means more than being undeceived: 'what a man has to learn through suffering is not this or that particular thing, but the knowledge of the limitations of humanity, of the absoluteness of the barrier which separates him from the divine. It is ultimately a religious insight—that kind of insight which gave birth to Greek tragedy. Thus experience is experience of human finitude. The truly experienced man is one who is aware of this, who knows that he is master neither of time nor of the future ...'.[31] Understanding is, then, an exploration of the dimensions of human finitude.

[30] Ibid., p. 319.
[31] Ibid., p. 320.

The question that now arises is: how do we proceed? What is meant by such openness to the past and how is it realized? Gadamer here draws on the 'logic of question and answer' developed by R. G. Collingwood as a critique of his 'realist' philosophical contemporaries of the Oxford *entre deux guerres*. Collingwood's own account of this is given in his *Autobiography*, and, as he relates it, it grew out of his twin concerns as a historian (especially as a archaeologist) and a philosopher. Collingwood begins by observing that archaeology is not a matter of digging up a historical site to see what can be found: all that happens if you do is that you find a lot of historical objects. You only begin to find out anything of real significance if you are digging for *something*, if you have formulated sufficiently precise and appropriate questions to which you are trying to find answers. And the difficult part of this process is asking the questions: finding the answers is relatively easy. The truth is not simply found by looking for it, but by asking questions and trying to find answers. Not that there is anything new about this: Plato's view of philosophy as dialogue witnesses to the fact that truth is found by a process of question and answer. 'When Plato described thinking as a "dialogue of the soul with itself", he meant (as we know from his own dialogues) that it was a process of question and answer, and that of these two elements the primacy belongs to the questioning activity, the Socrates within us.'[32] So when we seek to understand a literary text, its meaning is to be seen not as something that inheres in it which can be read off or elicited with greater or less difficulty: rather, understanding a text means understanding the question to which the writer is giving an answer. The first step is to attempt to reconstruct the question to which the text is giving an answer: and this process draws on all the resources that would be used by historical criticism. This approach cuts no Gordian knots; it opens to us no easy way to understanding. But as we seek to understand, we must go beyond mere reconstruction: we cannot avoid thinking about what was unquestioningly accepted by our author and so not thought about, and drawing this into the context of question and answer. As Gadamer puts it, 'The understanding of the world of tradition always requires that the reconstructed question be set

---

[32] *An Autobiography* (London, 1939), p. 35.

within the openness of its questionableness, that is, that it merge with the question that tradition is for us'[33]—we find in the process of seeking to understand that it is not simply a matter of our putting questions to the tradition, but of our being subject to questioning by that tradition itself. As we 'make the text speak', we hear what it has to say, and what it has to say, as we hear it, addresses us and calls us into question. If we are not open to that, we are not open to understanding. The process of reconstruction can be seen as an end in itself, as a way of entering the mind of the author and re-creating his thought after the manner of Dilthey. This shuts us off from the possibility of hearing the tradition addressing us. But if we are open to the tradition addressing us, then the possibility of historical knowledge being a closed body of facts or information is excluded. Such 'closed' history is replaced by 'open' history.

Collingwood never developed his 'logic of question and answer' in any very systematic way: it is not always clear what he has in mind. Sometimes we do seem to be veering off in the manner of Dilthey. But when he speaks of his experience as a teacher of philosophy, we see how the logic of question and answer in practice allowed the writings of the past to speak in the present:

Thus the history of philosophy, which my 'realist' friends thought a subject without philosophical significance, became for me a source of unfailing, and strictly philosophical, interest and delight ... But, of course, it was no longer a 'closed' subject. It was no longer a body of facts which a very, very learned man might know, or a very, very big book enumerate, in their completeness. It was an 'open' subject, an inexhaustible fountain of problems, old problems re-opened and new problems formulated that had not been formulated until now ... And if anybody had objected that in what I call 'open' history one couldn't see the wood for the trees, I should have answered, who wants to? A tree is a thing to look at; but a wood is not a thing to look at, it is a thing to live in.[34]

Behind much of Gadamer's reflection about the nature of understanding lies a basic analogy with the understanding that is sought and found in *conversation*. The different ways of seeking

---

[33] *Truth and Method*, p. 337.
[34] *An Autobiography*, pp. 75-6.

understanding can be seen to be analogous to different ways of engaging with a person in conversation. The first kind of engagement Gadamer considers is an engagement that does not really allow a conversation to develop at all. The other person is simply an object for me: I am observing him, and the 'conversation' that takes place is simply another context in which I can observe him. As a result of such observation I try and categorize him, determine what sort of a person he is, and predict his behaviour. Morally this way of proceeding is ultimately improper, for I am not treating the other as an 'end' (in Kant's sense) at all. This sort of 'conversation' is, Gadamer suggests, analogous to the procedure of the social sciences: people are its object of study, but they are treated as units which operate under laws that are to be discovered. The sort of 'objectivity' sought here is very close to the sort of objectivity promised by the scientific method.

Another sort of conversation, a real conversation this time, is made possible when I recognize that other as a person, and do not use my engagement with him as a means for extending my knowledge of human nature. But I can still use this relationship established in conversation as a means for seeking to 'understand' the other person. I am not directly interested in what he says, I am not listening to *what* he is saying: I am trying to 'read between the lines', I am trying to divine what he 'really' thinks and feels. I am trying to understand him better than he understands himself. I recognize his personhood, but I am trying to withdraw my own personhood from the relationship. This is the sort of thing that goes on in a 'therapeutic' conversation—with a 'counsellor' or with a psychiatrist. The counsellor is trying to get his client (as he calls him) to talk: he is trying to get him to express things he either does not want to say or is not really aware of. And through this insight into his client, he hopes to be able to help him. But another way of putting it would be to say that the counsellor is seeking to exercise power over his client (for his own good, of course). The client's own personhood is recognized, but the relationship is being manipulated by the counsellor, whose own personhood is not engaged in the conversation. This sort of conversation is, Gadamer suggests, analogous to the approach of what we call 'historical consciousness', which tries to reconstruct the historical context of the author and so get inside his skin, think his thought for him, and thus attain an understanding of the author that ideally transcends the author's own understanding of himself. The therapeutic motive (which may be an adequate justification for the procedure of the counsellor) is not present here, and in seeking to elide his own historical reality the one in search of understanding is, in effect, ignoring it. 'Historical consciousness knows about the otherness of the other, about the past in its otherness ... but by claiming to transcend its own conditionedness completely in its knowing of the other, it is involved in a false dialectic appearance, since it is actually seeking to master, as it were, the past.'[35]

But there is a further sort of conversation, an utterly genuine conversation this time, when I not only recognize the otherness of another, but also recognize his claim over me and listen to what he has to say to me. I am not trying to 'understand' him and thus dominate him; I am seeking to understand what he has to say, I am open to learning something from him. Here there is genuine listening, genuine openness to another. And this is analogous to the true way of seeking to understand the past, which Gadamer wants to commend. 'I must', he says, 'allow the validity of the claim made by tradition, not in the sense of simply acknowledging the past in its otherness, but in such a way that it has something to say to me. This too calls for a fundamental sort of openness. Someone who is open in this way to tradition sees that the historical consciousness is not really open at all, but rather, if it reads texts "historically" has always thoroughly smoothed them out beforehand, so that the criteria of our own knowledge can never be put in question by tradition.'[36]

Very early on in *Wahrheit und Methode* Gadamer remarks of the enterprise of his book: 'what makes the humanities into disciplines of learning (*Wissenschaften*, sciences) can be understood more easily from the tradition of the concept of *Bildung* than from the concept of method in modern science'.[37] The ways of trying to understand the endeavour of the humanities that Gadamer is taking to task, are ways that try and find some analogue within the study of the humanities to the

[35] *Truth and Method*, p. 323.
[36] Ibid., pp. 324-5. The whole discussion occupies pp. 321-5.
[37] Ibid., p. 18.

experimental method of the sciences: and the so-called historical-critical method is just such a method. And what is wrong is the attempt, which goes back to Descartes, to try and find a method, a technique, which will lead unerringly to the truth. Gadamer sets against the search for a method the tradition of *Bildung*. *Bildung*—or we could use the Greek word, *paideia*, education, though there is no word in English which corresponds with it very closely—is what one has to undergo in order to grow up, and also what it is that one grows up into. *Paideia* suggests etymologically the rearing of a child (*pais*), and in its use it means education and what this makes available to us: broadly, culture. *Bildung* suggests what is a central part of this process, form-ation.[38] Gadamer draws out some of the significance of *Bildung* in the introduction to *Wahrheit und Methode*. He refers to Vico, who in his defence of humanism (that is, a traditional, classical education) distinguishes two elements in it: common sense (which we have met already) and eloquence. Eloquence, he argues, means speaking well (*eu legein*) not just in the sense of rhetoric, but more significantly in the sense of knowing how to say the right thing in the right way at the right time. It is not mere 'cultivation': to say the right thing is to say the truth—not just, however, truth in some abstract, speculative sense, but the truth demanded by and appropriate to the particular situation. This requires not just knowledge of the truth, but sensitivity and discernment so that the truth is uttered in such a way that it is apprehended by those to whom it is uttered. Eloquence in this sense is a matter of practical wisdom, *phronesis*, in Aristotle's sense, as opposed to *sophia*, wisdom in the sense of universal truth. Eloquence, understood in this way as concerned with a sense for the truth in a particular situation, links up naturally with common sense, *sensus communis*. For the particular situation is always a social context which implies that we are thinking not just of a congeries of individuals, but of a group which has something in common. Common sense, then, is both what they have in common and a sensitivity for what men in any particular society have in common. Gadamer remarks in this context, 'there is something immediately obvious about groun-

---

[38] Gadamer notes the interesting fact that the origin of the word *Bildung* lies in German mystical literature in the notion of man as the image of God, *Bild Gottes*, and refers to the refashioning of man in that image: ibid., p. 11 and note 11.

ding literary and historical studies and the methods of the humanities in this idea of *sensus communis*. For their object, the moral and historical existence of man, is itself largely determined by the *sensus communis*. Thus an attempt based on universals, a reasoned proof, is not sufficient, because what is important is the circumstances. But this is only a negative formulation. The sense of the community mediates a unique positive knowledge.'[39]

By suggesting that *Bildung* occupy the place in the humanities which method occupies in the sciences, Gadamer means that initiation into the study of the humanities is not so much initiation into any techniques as into the tradition with which we are concerned in the humanities. Our primary aim is not to find a way that will enable us to achieve objectivity, but rather a sufficiently activated subjectivity, a sensitivity to our historical situation and all that has contributed to it— *Wirkungsgeschichte,* as Gadamer calls it—so that we can engage with the past in a fruitful dialogue. *Bildung,* then, fashions the individual so that he can benefit as fully as possible from his historical situation, whereas method attempts to transcend the situation of the observer so that he can record reality objectively. To quote Gadamer again: 'A person who imagines that he is free of prejudices, basing his knowledge on the objectivity of his procedures and denying that he is himself influenced by historical circumstances, experiences the power of the prejudices that unconsciously dominate him as a *vis a tergo*. A person who does not accept that he is dominated by prejudices will fail to see what is shown by their light.'[40] *Bildung* initiates a person into his prejudices, namely, all that which constitutes the perspective from which he can know anything at all in the moral world.

In this chapter we have looked at some of the ways in which one of the consequences of the Enlightenment, the divorce between the sciences and the humanities, has been understood. What we have found is, to some extent, further evidence for one of the contentions of chapter I: that the manifest success of the sciences has tended to distort our grasp of the variety of ways in which we apprehend the truth. But we have found too that 'our

---

[39] Ibid., p. 22.
[40] Ibid., p. 324.

lot, bequeathed to us by the Enlightenment'[41] is no simple, un-complicated heritage, and that it is by no means true that there is only one way of responding to its claims. From Vico onwards, as we have seen, there has been a resistance to the totalitarian claims of the scientific method, and it is at least as likely that theology will find its future within this resistance, as that it should concede these claims and make do with its 'lot'—quite apart from the fact that the defeat implied in accepting that our thought is determined by our cultural antecedents, is a defeat for thought itself. This chapter has sought to show that the prospect is much more open than some theologians are prepared to believe: if we venture forth into the realm thus disclosed to us, where shall we find ourselves?

[41] See introduction, p. xi.

III. SCIENCE AND MYSTERY

IT will be quite clear from the drift of the book so far that in my view theology has more in common with the humanities than it has with the sciences, and that therefore Gadamer's freeing of the humanities from the lure of the scientific method has consequences for theology, as well as for the humanities. It seems to be prima facie the case that the temptation to find a 'theological method' is likely to be an example of Steiner's 'fallacy of imitative form', just as it is in the humanities. In fact I would go further: it seems to me *quite obvious* that theology, as an academic discipline, finds its closest neighbours among the humanities rather than among the sciences: theologians conduct their academic work in libraries, not in laboratories; they read books, they do not conduct experiments.

Theology has, of course, traditionally been regarded as a science, indeed as the 'queen of the sciences', but in the sense of *scientia*, knowledge, as we mentioned earlier,[1] and not in our modern English sense. Aristotle regarded speculative, or theoretical, science (in contrast to 'practical' science) as the highest of the sciences, and theology as the noblest of the speculative sciences, for it was the study of the highest reality, the eternal and immutable being.[2] What we call the humanities were not, from this point of view, sciences at all, for they deal with what happens in history—with things, therefore, which have no necessity about them, which could very well have fallen out otherwise: of such accidental being there can be no true knowledge (*episteme*), it is not a fit subject for contemplation (*theoria*), it cannot form the subject-matter of a science. Within such a perspective, theology belonged with the sciences. For Aristotle, the object of theology could be established by considering what must be the case if there was to be knowledge of natural reality at all, that is, if physics, in his sense, were to be viable. Here was the origin of the cosmological argument for the existence of God, which established that there must be an

---

[1] See above, p. 13.
[2] See *Metaphysics*, 1026a, 1064b.

immutable, eternal being who could be the source of the change in natural reality, which was the object of the science of physics. Aristotle's tendency to see science as deductive, drawing true conclusions from indubitable principles, produced a hierarchy, the pinnacle of which was naturally theology, the study of the first principle of all, God. Aristotle's hierarchical pattern— whether mediated by later Platonism or as a direct influence— lay behind Patristic and medieval understanding of the place of theology in the map of human knowledge.

Clearly such an understanding of theology as a science could be—and has been—upset by at least two sorts of considerations. First, there is the story of the change in the notion of science, brought about by the growth of the experimental sciences. This involved a change from understanding science as a deductive method drawing conclusions from necessary premises, to seeing it as an inductive exercise proceeding by means of hypothesis and experiment—the change, in short, from an ancient to a modern concept of science. This is a familiar story involving the names of such as Grosseteste and Roger Bacon in the Middle Ages and leading up to the familiar protagonists of the Renaissance period such as Galileo and Francis Bacon. On such a modern understanding of science the hierarchy of the sciences vanishes, or at least is profoundly modified. What hierarchy remains is based not on the hierarchy of being, as Aristotle conceived it, but on the degree to which the scientific method is applicable in a strict sense: so physics tends, in this modern sense, to stand at the head of any scientific hierarchy, as the most exact of the exact sciences, as *the* science, *par excellence*. On the older view theology was the noblest of the sciences because it was the science of the highest being: on the modern view, the premiss of that implicit argument is taken away.

But in quite a different way the understanding of theology as the noblest of the sciences had always fitted awkwardly into the Judaeo-Christian tradition, according to which God is understood to have revealed himself within history. For whereas the Aristotelian notion suggests that knowledge of God is attained as we withdraw from temporal reality and ascend higher and higher in the scale of being, the Judaeo-Christian tradition directs us to what has happened, to temporal reality, and indeed to a particular sequence of events within temporal reality—the history of Israel culminating in the history of God Incarnate—as the *locus* for our knowledge of God. Certainly this challenge to the Aristotelian idea of theology as the highest science could be disguised by those who saw revelation in history as the revelation of absolutely certain propositions, which are gathered together in the Scriptures and provide the axiomatic basis for the science of Christian theology, the study of the Christian revelation. But even though this did mean that revealed theology could be regarded as a special department of theology, understood as the queen of the sciences, and so be found a place within the Aristotelian framework, none the less it fulfilled an odd role within that scheme. It did, however, mean that theology in fact—whatever the theory—concerned itself with texts and their meaning, that is, with what men had said and thought. It gave to history a dignity that perhaps it otherwise would not have had: the raw material of theology was not simply abstract thought, or even myths, but things that had happened. Much theology indeed, perhaps even the most important part of it so far as influence and impact went, concerned itself with what had happened and was happening: with God's dealings with Israel, and with the New Israel—as a whole, in Church history, and with particular individuals, in the lives of the saints.

So we see that in two ways the Aristotelian notion of theology as science has been challenged. On the one hand, by a change in the understanding of science from a deductive, theoretical exercise to an empirical study; and on the other, by the impact of something inherent in the Judaeo-Christian tradition itself, which sees God not simply as a metaphysical ultimate but as one who holds sway over history and is encountered in history. The force of the second possibility may not have always been felt (as we have suggested, it could be accommodated within the Aristotelian scheme) but sooner or later it was bound to be. Nor did the change in the understanding of science, a change which can be traced back to Roger Bacon, have its natural impact overnight: it was only with the seventeenth century and the dawn of the Enlightenment that its implications began to be realized.

But do we perhaps lose something in relinquishing the idea of theology as a science? Cannot perhaps the revision in the understanding of science that came about with the growth of experimental science give us a truer insight into the nature of theology *as a science?* Is there not something to be said for restoring theology to the realm of the sciences, if not to her erstwhile pre-eminent position as the 'queen of the sciences'? And, given the enormous respect in which the sciences are held nowadays, would it not be of considerable apologetic value if theology could be regarded as being genuinely 'scientific'? And is there not a further consideration, taking us back to the concerns of chapter I? There I spoke of a divide, a 'dissociation of sensibility', in our culture, and suggested that one of the elements in this dissociation is the way in which the claim of the scientific method to be the sole route to truth, with its consequence that truth is limited to the form of impersonal objectivity, has been too easily conceded by the humanities. But if we argue, as I have done, that the humanities are concerned with truth and that their way to this truth is radically different from the experimental method of the sciences, are we not promoting just such a divide in our understanding of the world, and therefore in our culture, that we have deplored in chapter I? May not the rediscovery of 'theological science' be the way to help us to heal this breach?

Certainly there have been attempts in recent times to find some common ground between theology and the sciences. The work of the late Ian Ramsey drew attention to ways of argument used by scientists which shed light on the methods of theological argument. The thrust of this seems to be apologetic: if the leaps in argument made by theologians are analogous to those made by scientists, then they cannot be rejected in principle, without at the same time casting doubt on the way in which scientists arrive at their conclusions (quite unthinkable in our culture with its reverence for scientific procedures). But something much more highly wrought is found in the work of Professor T. F. Torrance, especially in his work *Theological Science.*[3]

It is worth tracing the way in which Professor Torrance came to see the importance of drawing out a close analogy between theology and the exact sciences. In his book *Karl Barth: An Introduction to his Early Theology, 1910-31,*[4] Torrance lays great emphasis on the lectures Barth gave in Dortmund in 1929 under the title 'Schicksal und Idee in der Theologie' ('Fate and Idea in

[3] Oxford, 1969.
[4] London, 1962.

Theology'). It is in fact by exposition of these lectures that Torrance develops what was involved in the change in Barth's
thought from the dialectical theology of the twenties (which
began with his commentary on Romans) to the mature thinking which eventually bore fruit in his massive *Church Dogmatics*.
It is not usually noticed how original Torrance's reading
of Barth is here. The usual view (and one Barth himself seemed
to lend his weight to) is that the crucial turning-point in
Barth's thought is to be found in his book[5] on Anselm's proof for
the existence of God in the *Proslogion*. Torrance recognizes that
this book 'represents the decisive turning-point in his thinking',
but he sees it rather as 'the final point in his advance from
dialetical thinking to Church dogmatics'.[6] What was actually involved in this advance Torrance expounds by a lengthy discussion of the Dortmund lectures (which occupies pp. 149-80 of his
book). In these lectures Barth examines the relation of theology
to philosophy, first to a philosophy of realism (such as that
of Aristotle or St. Thomas Aquinas) and then to an idealist
philosophy (such as Hegel's). A realist philosophy, Barth
argues, seeks to lay bare the nature of reality, it seeks to elucidate
what is given. For such thought, 'God is ontologically and
noetically the fate of mankind'. The givenness of God for such
thought can be apprehended either within or without, and consequently this kind of thinking can develop in the direction of
pietism or rationalism: but at its centre is the assertion that God
is, the assertion of God's reality and actuality. However, Barth
observes, if such a theology is to remain theology, the God it
affirms must not be just any God, but the God of the Christian
Church, the God who is known where he has made himself
known: God is not just a given reality, there for man to discover,
rather he is one who reveals himself. The danger with a
philosophy of realism is that God may be reduced to the level of
fate, of an ultimate givenness holding sway over man's destiny.
Against this, theology has to proclaim that the God who reveals
himself in the Christian Church is not a God who is simply
given, but a living God, who reveals himself, One who comes.
  A philosophy of idealism, on the other hand, seeks *truth,* and

[5] Published in English as *Anselm: Fides Quaerens Intellectum* (London, 1960).
[6] *Karl Barth: An Introduction*, p. 182.

the danger here is that God will be apprehended as the ultimate 'beyond' of human thought: as a kind of ultimate limit towards which human thought is constantly approaching as it fashions more and more adequate syntheses of its knowledge and experience of the world. Here, Barth maintains, theology, if it is to remain a truly Christian theology, must insist on the essential place of *faith*, a faith which recognizes God as the Creator, rather than seeing God as the ultimate term in man's creative visions of reality. And such a faith demands obedience, obedience to God's revelation of himself. And so theology is less free than philosophy, for theology is bound to what God has revealed of himself; it is not free to make what it will of its own experience.

For Barth, philosophy, whether realist or idealist, is an enterprise of the human spirit, freely attempting to make sense of its perceptions and intuitions. A satisfactory philosophy is one that makes a satisfying synthesis of the perceptions of realism and the creative intuitions of idealism; it can do this by stressing one or the other, or by interpreting both these tendencies in the light of some third principle. But the art of theology is not such an art: the theologian is not to cultivate the creative freedom of the philosopher. Rather, the theologian stands before the Word of God, and sees in the Word One who comes, One who cannot be bound by the apprehensions of the one who hears the Word. This is the Word who says to him, 'Ye have not chosen me, but I have chosen you'. For Barth the presupposition of any true theological thought is the notion of divine election: the hearer of the Word is the elect—not primarily as an individual, but as a member of God's chosen people.

It is easy to see how Barth is here etching out the fundamental features of the understanding of theology that lies behind the *Church Dogmatics*. Torrance is surely right in drawing attention to these lectures as he seeks to expound what was involved in Barth's transition from dialetical theology to dogmatic theology. But what is interesting, and what concerns us most closely here, is Torrance's final comment in this discussion: 'As it has turned out, does not theology bear a closer comparison with an *exact science*, such as physics, which restricts its activities to the limits laid down by the nature of its concrete object, and develops a method in accordance with the nature of its object, bracketing it off from every world-view (either as an *a priori* condition or as an *a posteriori* product), and involving an open mind about what may lie beyond the limits of its own area of knowledge?'[7]

Barth himself did not pursue the parallel between theology and the exact sciences which Torrance suggests here. It is true that the opening pages of the *Church Dogmatics* are devoted to the notion of theology as 'science', but the German word translated 'science'—*Wissenschaft*—has a much broader meaning than the English word 'science' tends to have nowadays. To say that theology is a science means for Barth that it is a 'human effort after truth'; in making this claim theology 'confesses its solidarity with other efforts of this kind which to-day are united for good and all under this idea'.[8] But such 'solidarity' does not mean that theology has anything to learn from the methods of the other sciences, nor that it should seek inspiration from their procedures. Such 'solidarity' *does* mean that theology is reminded of the fact that it is a *human* endeavour: the fact that it concerns itself with the divine does not confer on it any superhuman insight or efficacy. This solidarity also means that the very existence of theology as an academic discipline (a description which perhaps conveys more exactly the nature of Barth's claims for theology) registers a 'necessary protest ... against the admittedly "heathen" general concept of science'. As Barth puts it: 'It can do neither its own most stalwart representatives, nor the university, any harm to be reminded, by the proximity of the theologian under the same roof, that the quasi-religious unconditionality of their interpretation of this concept of science is in practice not undisputed, that the tradition beginning with the name of Aristotle is at all events but one among others, and that, once for all, the Christian Church at least does not have Aristotle for its ancestor.' But Barth is not at all interested in pursuing analogies that might exist between theology and any other sciences; theology 'cannot allow itself to be taught by them the concrete meaning which that involves in its own case. As regards method it has nothing to learn in their school.'[9]

For Torrance, however, the suggestion he makes in comment on the theme of Barth's Dortmund lectures is one that he has

[7] Ibid., pp. 179-80.
[8] *Church Dogmatics*, I/1 (ET Edinburgh, 1936), p. 10.
[9] Ibid., p. 7.

taken up himself, and which he regards as shedding a great deal
of light on the nature of theology. A series of works, beginning
with his *Theological Science*, seeks to develop this insight. What we
find is not *simply* an attempt to assimilate theology to the exact
sciences; rather what we find is an attempt to derive some
illumination for the theological task from the way in which
modern science (and in particular modern physics) has had to
grapple with the problem of epistemology, that is, the problem of
understanding how knowledge is arrived at and what that
knowledge is. And there is light to be found here: in particular,
in Torrance's emphasis on the way science has been able to hold
on to the idea that it is concerned with objective knowledge and
yet has escaped from the naïvety of a crude empiricism. But in so
far as this is true, it seems to me only to mean that knowing in the
sciences, because it is a *human* activity, is much less unlike
understanding in the humane disciplines than the early protagonists of the scientific method seem to have thought. The
illumination that Torrance brings to the theological task is
mainly oblique: for the simple reason, so it seems to me, that the
procedures of theology *are* the procedures of the humanities, not
those of the sciences ('libraries, not laboratories'). Experiment
is crucial and central to the sciences (even if in some of the
sciences much more time is actually spent in thought: the
construction of theories and the theoretical examination of their
implications). Torrance is perfectly aware of this:

Natural objects, as we have seen, have to be the objects of our cognition
when we know them, but it is only out of pure Grace that God gives
Himself to be the object of our knowing and thinking. It is upon this
that there rests the essential difference between the kind of enquiry apposite in theology and that apposite in the other sciences, and also upon
the kind of verification or demonstration required. The experimental
investigation through man-made controls, and the corresponding
demonstration offered by making things work as we stipulate, are
scientifically inappropriate to the living God, for it would not be the
Lord God but an idol that could come under our power like that, and it
would not be theology but magic that could conjure up and manipulate
'the divine' like that.[10]

_____

[10] *Theological Science*, p. 299.

The experimental method, then, has for Torrance no place in theology: so at the heart of the matter theology is *not* like the exact sciences. The reason Torrance gives for this difference between theology and the other sciences is that theology is concerned with God's giving himself to us through *grace,* whereas science is concerned with natural objects. But in offering this reason—a perfectly valid and wholly appropriate reason for marking off theology from the sciences—Torrance goes too far too quickly. It is not only where we have to do with grace in the strict, theological sense that an experimental method is inappropriate, but also when we have to do with men and women, with persons. In the moral realm too, as well as in the realm of the divine, the experimental method is inappropriate. That theology has to do with God's gracious self-revelation will distinguish theology from all other forms of knowledge, but that distinction will not coincide with the distinction implied by the propriety or lack of propriety of the experimental method: that distinction runs between the natural sciences and the humanities, and should thus lead even Torrance himself to class theology among the humanities.

If this criticism of Torrance's position is accepted, then it must mean that Torrance is mistaken in the fundamental thrust of his enterprise. But it does not mean that there is not much to be learnt from the kind of considerations he raises in the course of his books. His analysis of, for example, the way in which theologians have been unconsciously influenced by different notions of space may indeed lead us to see a way through various controversies which have occupied theologians in the past. This, however, seems to me to be quite independent of Torrance's claim that modern science supports one view of space rather than another. This claim is not really an essential part of his case: the quite genuine weight that it carries is extraneous to the point of substance. Modern science lends its *prestige* to this view of space: and this has apologetic value which Torrance is right to perceive, and not obviously wrong in wishing to exploit. St. Thomas Aquinas, in the first question of his *Summa Theologiae,* argued that though in sacred theology, *sacra doctrina,* conclusions could only be reached by considerations that themselves belong to theology, other bodies of knowledge could often provide 'extraneous and probable arguments', which it was legitimate for theology to utilize. By analogy, Torrance's appeal to modern science provides 'extraneous and probable arguments' which he is not wrong to use.

But if our main criticism is accepted, it means that if the theologian is to look over his shoulder at other academic disciplines at all, it is rather to the humanities that he should look, and in doing so should not be looking there for any analogy to the scientific method, but rather for a different way of knowing that does not rely on method and technique. None the less, left like that, we would be settling for a fundamental divide in our way of apprehending the truth, which might well be potentially disastrous. Perhaps at this point we ought to pause and wonder whether we have not allowed ourselves to accept too readily a characterization of the scientific method that amounts more or less to a caricature.

In speaking of the scientific method, I have had in mind the considerations raised in chapter I in the discussion of the idea that came to prominence in the wake of the Renaissance: that the way to truth was to break with tradition and traditional ways of understanding, and instead to start from scratch following a method that analysed our experience into its components and then sought to establish these basic bricks of our experience (see above, p. 7). The idea is that we start from a state of ignorance (formalized by Descartes in his method of universal doubt) and then seek to build up a body of objective knowledge, established by means of observation and experiment. It is a confessedly iconoclastic method: we pull down the edifice that we have received from tradition, and try to replace it with something we have established for ourselves. The possible subjectivism implied in this way of putting it is avoided by an insistence that the results of the experimental method are something that is the same for all, since it is a principle of the scientific method that experiments be repeatable by different experimenters, and this eliminates any possible personal bias in the observation of the experimenter. So we have here a way of seeking knowledge which systematically doubts and rejects tradition, and which seeks a knowledge which is in principle independent of the one who knows it. This method had been successful in the sense that in many areas of knowledge misunderstanding and error have been cleared away, and a true understanding of the state of affairs promoted. But this may not mean that it is a *complete* way of developing human knowledge, only that it is effective within its limits.

Take the place of tradition, for example. The scientific approach is to mistrust tradition. In his Hulsean Lectures,[11] F. J. A. Hort, a tireless and careful scholar in such matters as the text of the New Testament and the history of the primitive and early Church, and also something of a natural scientist, remarked, apropos of the Church's tradition but making a wider claim, 'perhaps those who are themselves best exercised in unwearied and courageous search will be the readiest to profess how much they have been helped throughout towards clear and dispassionate vision by the gracious pressure of some legitimate tradition or other authority, into the limits of whose jurisdiction they had seldom occasion to enquire'.[12] Hort argues that the claim that the divine revelation is the truth places theological knowledge alongside other forms of knowledge, and he draws out lightly a parallel between theological truth (the 'truth of revelation') and the truth ascertained by the growth of the natural sciences (the 'truth of discovery'). He insists that they are not utterly different kinds of truth that cannot be compared with one another: 'nor is the character of truth changed by the form in which it is originally acquired: it is no merely verbal bond which unites truth of revelation to truth of discovery',[13] or again: 'once more, theological truth is not divided from other truth by the inscrutable nature of its subject matter'. He points out that the contrast between truth of revelation and truth of discovery merely brings out a polarity in the human grasping of truth that is necessarily implicit in it. There cannot be pure truth of revelation: for to apprehend a truth which is received is to relate it to what we know already, to make it one's own. But neither can there be pure truth of discovery: for no one starts from scratch, we take for granted a body of learning that has been handed down to us, we *trust* those from whom we learn, and those from whom they learnt. 'Truth of discovery is received by every one except the discoverer as much from without as if it were

[11] Published as *The Way, The Truth, The Life* (London, 2nd edn. reprinted 1897).

[12] Ibid., p. 87. It is interesting to note that in the same year as Hort gave his Hulsean Lectures (1871) he was also an examiner in the Natural Sciences Tripos at Cambridge.

[13] Ibid., p. 75.

revealed. Truth of revelation remains inert till it has been appropriated by a human working of recognition which it is hard to distinguish from that of discovery.' Hort draws attention to the danger of thinking that because much of the advance in knowledge since the Renaissance has been by criticism and rejection of traditions discovered to be false, it follows that tradition has no place in our knowing, and that we should accept only what we have proved for ourselves. The task is impossible; but more dangerously, the attitude behind such a determination is self-frustrating: 'in knowledge as in all else he labours in vain to be independent: he is most himself when he receives most, and most freely acknowledges that he receives'.[14] In a long passage Hort draws out the limiting and stultifying effects of a fundamental mistrust of tradition:

The subjection to early teaching was or should have been no bondage at all, but the one indispensable condition of a strong and timely growth. Without the regimen of a fixed and prescribed form of truth the faculties run riot in premature licence, and gain nothing but disablement for effective operation hereafter. Nor is the influence of a tempered authority in matters of truth less salutary after the first or second probation is over. The air is thick with bastard traditions which carry us captive unawares while we seem to ourselves to be exercising our freedom and our instinct for truth. The traditions of the hour or the age are as indubitably external to us, and as little founded of necessity on freshly perceived truth, as any traditions of the past. The danger of them lies in their disguise. The single negative fact that they make war on some confessed tradition prevents us from discovering that they too draw their force no less from an authority, until it is too late and we have lost or damaged that power of independent vision which is but braced and harmonized by a known and honoured tradition.[15]

There is much in this passage that will remind the reader of ideas of Gadamer discussed above, only here there is no animus against science and the scientific method, rather a calm perception that the nurturing value of tradition for any real advance in knowledge holds for all understanding of the truth. When Hort goes on to develop the positive, personal qualities needed in one who is in pursuit of the truth, we find themes emerging, which have also been seen in Gadamer, in particular the idea of the in-

---

[14] Ibid., p. 78.
[15] Ibid., pp. 91-2.

crease in knowledge as a process of undeception, and the importance of discipline and learning—what Gadamer unites in the
word *Bildung*. So Hort continues:

> The perception of truth depends as much on the state of him that
> desires to perceive as on the objects that are presented to his view. No
> slight or swift or uniform process will enable any one to master the
> mere art of discerning truth from false appearance. But, not to speak of
> this most needful and most various mental preparation, there is
> another condition which is never forgotten with impunity. The more
> we know of truth, the more we come to see how manifold is the opera-
> tion by which we take hold of it. It is not reached through one organ but
> through many. No single faculty, if indeed there be any single
> faculties, can arrogate a right to exclude from the domain of truth what
> cannot be readily subjected to its own special action. It may be that no
> element of our compound nature is entirely shut out from taking part
> in knowledge. It is at all events certain that the specially mental powers
> will never be able to judge together in rightful relation when the nature
> as a whole is disordered by moral corruption. There is no evil passion
> cherished, no evil practice followed, which does not cloud or distort our
> vision whenever we look beyond the merest abstract forms of things.
> There is a truth within us, to use the language of Scripture, a perfect
> inward ordering as of a transparent crystal, by which alone the faithful
> image of truth without us is brought within our ken. Not in vain said
> the Lord that it is the pure in heart, they whose nature has been sub-
> dued from distraction into singleness, who shall see God; or, we may
> add, who shall see the steps of the ladder by which we may mount to
> God.
>
> The stedfast and prescient pursuit of truth is therefore itself a moral
> and spiritual discipline.[16]

This vision of the qualities required in one who dedicates
himself to the pursuit of truth applies to anyone who thus dedicates himself. There could be no 'method' which would lead one
to the truth without making any demands—and most stringent
demands—on the one thus led. Hort has too a vision of the way
in which the growth of the natural sciences will contribute to
theological truth. This vision is only sketched out, but two points
emerge clearly enough. First, the growing knowledge of the
natural order (what Hort calls the 'younger' knowledge) will
complement and, as it were, act as ballast to man's aspira-
tion to know the eternal God. This latter knowledge, developed

[16] Ibid., pp. 92-3.

throughout the history of the Church (and so called the 'elder' knowledge), has had a tendency to be purely speculative, in a pejorative sense, building imaginative structures based on only hints and guesses as to what might really be the case ('soaring imaginations calling themselves knowledge ... but borrowing from ascertained truth no more than suggestions'—something that Hort prophetically foresaw would be again one of the consequences of intoxicating draughts of the fresh knowledge made available by the sciences). As Hort put it, 'The elder knowledge was itself imperfect, and always tending to become the shadow of a once substantial knowledge, so long as the younger was unborn.'[17] But secondly, Hort saw another, more exact, influence on theology of the 'younger' knowledge which underlines and elaborates on man's place in the world; whereas the 'elder' knowledge tended to set man over against nature, so the 'younger' knowledge sees man as a part of nature. This means that the implications of the Christian doctrine of the resurrection of the body can be more clearly seen, and be seen in their full importance: for the body is certainly a part of the world which is being explored by the sciences. So Hort says, 'To deny the redemption of the body is to deny Christ and to relapse into heathen despair; and the redemption of the body carries with it the redemption of the world to which it belongs. As we can seldom bathe ourselves in the freshness of living things without coming forth with purified and brightened hearts, even such let us believe may be the effect of the truth of nature on our thoughts of God Himself.'[18]

This last paragraph has been something of a digression from our main theme, which is the *kind* of study theology is, rather than its content; but it nevertheless helps to show that even if we decide that theology has nothing to gain from an analogy with the exact sciences, this does not mean that the sciences have no relevance at all for theology. For it must be the case that the world revealed to us by the sciences (in so far as they give us a *true* vision of the world, rather than a merely *useful* one) will have some bearing on the theologian's articulation of his vision. But a theologian does not become scientific merely by embracing the world-view of scientists; in so far as their vision of the world is true, it is merely rational to accept it.

[17] Ibid., p. 80.
[18] Ibid., p. 84.

From Hort there emerges a very positive attitude to the growth of the sciences which yet sees the pursuit of the scientist as part of the common human pursuit for truth, and as not fundamentally different from it in kind. Emphasis is laid on the importance of tradition; while the objectivity required of the one who is seriously dedicated to the truth is seen not as an impersonal elision of the observer, but rather in moral terms as a growth in wisdom and selflessness. Nor is there any reliance on some 'method' which holds the key of knowledge, rather there is an awareness of the manifoldness of the truth and of our perception of it. Something similar is found in quite a different writer, and in quite a different, more strictly epistemological, context, in the works of Michael Polanyi. Even less than in the case of Hort can we suspect in Polanyi any sort of animus against the sciences, so it is significant that he develops an interpretation of what is involved in knowing and understanding that questions all attempts to make of the scientific method a privileged way of knowing, utterly different from and more reliable than other human ways of understanding. The particular element of Polanyi's thought we shall concentrate on is his notion of the 'tacit dimension'.

At the heart of Polanyi's insight here is his recognition of what one might call the mysteriousness of our engagement with the outside world. The kind of empiricism that often underpins the scientific or experimental method assumes that our perception of the external world is relatively straightforward and unproblematic: that we simply register impressions from the external world and organize them by a process of interpretation. Polanyi's point is that in much of our perception of the external world, what we perceive is often unspecifiable in detail. We recognize one another's faces, yet are quite unable to specify what it is that we are recognizing: but that does not, of course, cast doubt on our ability to recognize one another. In some mysterious manner the details we are aware of—the shape of the nose, the look of the eyes, the way a person carries himself, and so on—are fused by us into a form, a *Gestalt*, that is for us unique and instantly recognizable. If we attempt to attend to the detail, we often miss the more elusive total impression that we discern but cannot explain. Polanyi's point here is akin to something Berdyaev remarked on in his book *Solitude and Society*: 'As a matter of fact, our knowledge of another's body is very limited. We can only perceive it superficially and can have no idea of what goes on within it; but our knowledge of other people's psychic life is infinitely greater; we are better able to grasp it and to penetrate more immediately into it ... The vision of another person's countenance, the expression of his eyes, can often be a spiritual revelation. The eyes, the gestures, the words—all these are infinitely more eloquent of a man's soul than of his body.'[19] Polanyi gives several other examples of this phenomenon. The diagnosis of a disease, for instance, is something that is often unspecifiable in detail. One learns by experience to recognize the pattern of symptoms, while finding it difficult to explain in what the pattern consists—difficult to explain, because it is not a matter of listing symptoms, which may not all be present on each occasion. Knowing whether the absence of a particular symptom is significant or not is a matter of experience. Polanyi illustrates this by a story: 'A few years ago a distinguished psychiatrist demonstrated to his students a patient who was having a mild fit of some kind. Later the class discussed the question whether this had been an epileptic or a hystero-epileptic seizure. The matter was finally decided by the psychiatrist: "Gentlemen," he said, "you have seen a true epileptic seizure. I cannot tell you how to recognize it; you will learn this by more extensive experience." '[20]

This pattern of knowing is very generally true. Polanyi gives examples from the performance of skills, the proper use of sensory organs, the mastery of tools and probes, the use of language. In all these cases we find that a man is able to do something, for instance, riding a bicycle or swimming, by integrating a vast number of particular perceptions, without understanding why what he is doing achieves the desired result. He turns corners on a bicycle without at all knowing that this depends more on the way he tilts the bicycle than on his turning of the front wheel. One learns by experience to behave in a certain way, to respond to what is happening sensitively and effectively. Visual perception too is not a matter of simply registering visual sensation. We select, organize, and integrate what lies in our visual field. Two people see the same bird: one simply sees a bird, the other sees what sort of a bird it is. In one sense they have

[19] London, 1938, p. 109.
[20] *Knowing and Being* (London, 1969), p. 123.

each seen the same thing, in another sense they have not. The one who has seen only a bird may have the dimmest awareness of its colour and markings, the one who has recognized what sort of a bird it is will have noticed all this in the act of seeing it. We say that one of them 'knows what to look for': in looking he is, as it were, asking questions and looking for answers.

What Polanyi is suggesting when he draws out the complex nature of visual perception is very close to the logic of question and answer discussed above in Collingwood. But neither the one who sees just a bird, nor the one who sees a particular bird, need have any understanding of how the sensory organ, the eye, operates: in seeing, they are making use of a vast number of particulars, some of which they are utterly unaware of. They see because they have learnt by experience to discern things in their visual field: and one has more experience than the other and sees more. Polanyi points out too that, in the way we use tools and probes, what we perceive is not what we experience through our senses. A rower pulling at an oar feels the resistance of the water, not the various sense impressions in his hands. In using a paper knife, we feel the paper of the envelope being cut, not the sense impressions in our hands. A blind man using a stick feels not the impact of the stick on his hand, but what the end of his stick is knocking against. Again, in using a language we, as it were, see through the words to what they mean: we hear the meaning, not just the vocal sounds—something that is very apparent, by contrast, when we hear words in a language we do not understand.

Polanyi interprets this by distinguishing between what he calls subsidiary awareness, and focal awareness. Many of the particulars we perceive are not the focus of our awareness, rather they point to that focus. In a very simple case, we might think of someone pointing something out to us with his finger. We see the finger, but we are not looking at it, we are following it and looking at what it is pointing to. We have subsidiary awareness of the finger, and focal awareness of what the finger is pointing at. In most of our perception we integrate a vast variety of things subsidiarily perceived into focal awareness of what we are perceiving. And we do this by bringing to our perception a whole range of anticipations we have learnt by experience. We bring a kind of interpretative framework within which we seek to interpret our conceptions: and this framework is *tacit*, it is something we have learnt by experience and *cannot* make wholly explicit. For Polanyi all knowledge is either *tacit* or *rooted in tacit knowledge*. It is not simply objective, but knowledge which has been grasped and understood by a person. So Polanyi speaks of 'personal knowledge' or 'personal knowing'.

This conception of knowledge as personal knowing departs in two closely related respects from the ideal of a strictly justifiable knowledge. It accredits man's capacity to acquire knowledge even though he cannot specify the grounds of his knowing, and it accepts the fact that his knowing is exercised within an accidentally given framework that is largely unspecifiable. These two acceptances are correlated within the effort of integration which achieves knowing. For this effort subsidiarily relies on the one hand, on stimuli coming from outside, from all parts of our body and from tools or instruments assimilated to our body, and on the other hand, on a wide range of linguistic pointers which bring to bear our pre-conceptions—based on past experience—on the interpretation of our subject matter. The structure of knowing, revealed by the limits of specifiability, thus fuses our subsidiary awareness of the particulars belonging to our subject matter with the cultural background of our knowing.[21]

What we have in Polanyi is an analysis of what is involved in knowing that calls into question some of the simplifications underlying the idea that the scientific method, the experimental method, is the way of moving from ignorance and error to objective knowledge. Any movement is largely a movement between explicit and tacit knowledge, and that not a one-way movement either, as if the idea was to move from tacit to explicit knowledge, for, as Polanyi points out, explicit knowledge has to become tacit if it is to be fruitful: 'The speed and complexity of tacit integration far exceeds in its own domain the operations of explicit inference. This is how intuitive insight may arrive at unaccountable conclusions in a flash.'[22] Polanyi gives as an example the way in which the explicit knowledge contained in a car-driving manual only becomes useful and effective as it becomes tacit: 'the text of the manual is shifted to the back of the driver's mind, and is transposed almost entirely into the tacit operations of a skill'.[23] Knowledge is, for Polanyi, much more a personal

[21] Ibid., pp. 133-4.
[22] Ibid., pp. 144-5.
[23] Ibid., p. 144.

orientation towards reality than any kind of objective account of it: the attempt to achieve some objective description of reality, or a part of it, is an aspect of what is involved in my gaining a genuine orientation of my own towards reality, rather than the end in view. Here again, as in the last chapter, we are discerning some of the truth of Kierkegaard's assertion that 'Truth is Subjectivity'—an assertion which is utterly misunderstood if it is taken to mean that there is no objective truth at all.

One of the consequences of Polanyi's understanding of knowing as personal knowing is that we can begin to see more clearly how all knowing is one, all truth is one. Polanyi uses Dilthey's idea of knowledge as 'indwelling' as a way of explaining how it is that we know:

> I have shown how our subsidiary awareness of our body is extended to include a stick, when we feel our way by means of the stick. To use language in speech, reading and writing, is to extend our bodily equipment and become intelligent human beings. We may say that when we learn to use language, or a probe, or a tool, and thus make ourselves aware of these things as we are of our body, we *interiorize* these things and *make ourselves dwell in them*. Such extensions of ourselves develop new faculties in us; our whole education operates in this way; as each of us interiorizes our cultural heritage, he grows into a person seeing the world and experiencing life in terms of this outlook. [24]

But Dilthey's notion of indwelling was developed to explain how different understanding in the humanities is from understanding in the sciences. Polanyi's use of indwelling to explain how we know in the sciences, or indeed at all, suggests a greater unity of knowledge than Dilthey suspected. Polanyi himself put his point thus:

> Tacit knowing now appears as an act of *indwelling* by which we gain access to a new meaning. When exercising a skill we literally dwell in the innumerable muscular acts which contribute to its purpose, a purpose which constitutes their joint meaning. Therefore, since all understanding is tacit knowing, all understanding is achieved by indwelling. The idea developed by Dilthey and Lipps, that we can know human beings and works of art only by indwelling, can thus be justified. But we see now also that these authors were mistaken in distinguishing indwelling from observation as practised in the natural

[24] Ibid., p. 148.

sciences. The difference is only a matter of degree: indwelling is less deep when observing a star than when understanding men or works of art. The theory of tacit knowing establishes a continuous transition from the natural sciences to the study of the humanities.[25]

This provokes two observations. First, that to look to the sciences to find some light for the theological task is needless. For what we have now found is that the way of understanding in the sciences is fundamentally the same as the way of understanding in the humanities. It is a popular misconception that the sciences have discovered some key to knowledge denied to the humanities (and to divinity, or theology): the ultimate pattern of knowing is one. Indeed, Polanyi's bow towards Dilthey suggests that what is really involved in knowing is better grasped in the humanities than in the sciences, even if in the latter there has been in recent centuries a kind of measurable progress that we do not find in the humanities. But secondly, there is in this pattern of knowing which is emerging, whether we look at the thought of Gadamer in the last chapter, or of Polanyi in the present chapter, something that is, or ought to be, familiar to theologians, for it is the pattern of understanding we find above all in the theologians of the classic period of the Church's history—the period of the Ecumenical Councils and of the Fathers. For the Fathers knowledge of God, and of his love for us in Jesus Christ, could only be found within the tradition of the Church. 'Habere iam non potest Deum patrem qui ecclesiam non habet matrem': he who no longer has the Church for his mother cannot have God as his Father.[26]

If we look at the role of tradition in our coming to know God we find in the Fathers a pattern reminiscent of what we have already noticed in Gadamer and Polanyi. Participation in the tradition of the Church meant for the Fathers acceptance of the Church's rule of faith, acceptance of the framework of preconceptions within which Scripture and one's own experience of grace could be interpreted as furthering the understanding of God. This tradition was essentially *non-specifiable,* or if specifiable, not simply by an indication of specific doctrines, but primarily as the bond of unity, the bond of love,

[25] Ibid., p. 160.
[26] *St. Cyprian: De Ecclesiae Catholicae Unitate,* 6 (ed. M. Bévenot SJ, Oxford, 1971: p. 66).

which established the Church as the Body of Christ. As the Church reflected on the notion of tradition, it developed (as we shall see in more detail in the next chapter) a notion of what we might call, following Polanyi, a *tacit dimension* in which our knowledge of God is rooted. The Patristic doctrine of tradition might well be paraphrased in the language of Polanyi by saying that all knowledge of God in Christ is either the tacit knowledge of tradition or rooted in such tacit knowledge.

The notion of the tacit has deeper resonance within the Fathers' thought, however, than in the thought of Polanyi. In them the tacit is interpreted as silence, the silence of presence, the presence of God who gives himself to the soul who waits on him in silence. The silence of the tacit makes immediate contact with the silence of prayer: and prayer is seen in the Fathers to be, as it were, the amniotic fluid in which our knowledge of God takes form. Participation in the tradition of the Church implies participation in a life of love, of loving devotion to God and loving care of our neighbour. Participation in the tradition is indeed a *moral* activity: it implies a growing attentiveness to Our Lord, and a growing likeness to him. In other words, the Fathers understand the place of what we have called, following Gadamer, *paideia* in making us into those who are capable of knowing God, or rather in making us receptive to God's revelation of himself in Jesus Christ. Hort's assertion that 'the perception of truth depends as much on the state of him that desires to perceive as on the objects that are presented to his view' is axiomatic for the Fathers.

The idea that theology must work within the alleged heritage of the Enlightenment now looks much less compelling. For it is just this heritage that is the object of the criticism of Gadamer and Polanyi. And it is not simply that theology is free to return to a way of approach that was so fruitful in the early centuries; more than that, we find not only that a common pattern emerges from the criticism of Gadamer and Polanyi, despite their very different starting-points, but that this common pattern has a striking resemblance to the pattern that we can discern in the approach of the Fathers of the Church. The way of much theology since the Enlightenment—with only a few notable exceptions, in England those who drank deep of the wine of the Fathers, such as the fathers of the Oxford Movement, and such as Hort—is seen to be based on assumptions about how we come to knowledge that are being rendered increasingly incredible and naïve.

I have maintained both that the lure of the scientific method has been damaging to the humanities (and to theology), and that this lure has led to a very one-sided understanding of truth and how we can know truth, a one-sidedness I have associated with what has been called a 'dissociation of sensibility' in our culture. None the less, science has been very successful: it has advanced in a way quite unlike anything found in the humanities, and indeed those branches of the humanities that have known some progress have usually progressed by finding within themselves some part of their task that can be regarded as scientific. The idea that the success of the sciences is itself one-sided, and becoming increasingly dangerous in that it is dictating the kind of things that can be regarded as true, is an idea we find in Polanyi, and his development of the notion of personal knowing is an attempt to prevent this intoxication with a one-sided successfulness.[27] But what I want to suggest in the rest of this chapter, is that the progress of the sciences (and the quasi-sciences) is the result of their developing (in a remarkable and impressive way) one side, one dimension, of the human faculty of rationality, and that while this dimension is present in the disciplines of the humanities (and theology), the heart of these disciplines is found in another (and deeper) dimension.

One of the ways in which reason operates is by solving problems. In his confrontation with reality man isolates certain problems and seeks solutions. Mathematics represents this faculty of reason perhaps at its point of most acute development: it is mathematics that has enabled the sciences to pose problems in such a way that they are rendered soluble. Put like that, it may sound very humdrum, but this is far from the case. The solving of problems involves the exercise of imagination in posing the problems in such a way that they suggest ways of solution. Though methods can be developed here, what is much more important is a kind of imaginative insight into the pattern the problem presents. And indeed in the solution itself one looks for order, symmetry, even, one might say, for elegance, and not simply for any sort of answer. The pure mathematician, the pure

---

[27] See his article 'The Two Cultures', reprinted in *Knowing and Being*, pp. 40-6.

problem-solver, does not at all see his task in utilitarian terms, but often rather in aesthetic categories (see, for example, G. H. Hardy's famous defence of the pure mathematician's vocation in *A Mathematician's Apology*). None the less, the problems are there to be solved, and once solved they are of no further interest, except in so far as they suggest approaches to further problems. The sciences advance by being able to isolate problems that are capable of solution in terms of the position the science has at that time reached. Looking at problems too soon is not the way to advance, and looking at problems too late is either folly, or the menial function of tidying up what is already known in principle anyway. There is a very real notion of advance and progress: problems solved represent knowledge achieved and form the basis for further advance. It seems to me that it is the realization that science is this sort of activity that has led to the success of the sciences: and the notion of advance (with the implication that the past has been left behind) is part and parcel of this notion.

The humanities are not basically like this at all. They are characterized by a continual returning to the great figures of the past. Philosophers continue to discuss Plato, for instance; the problems that he raised are not problems that admit of the kind of solution which would enable us to leave them behind and pass on to other problems. The notion of advance is much less easy to sustain. Of course, there *is* a certain sort of advance: there is a place for the kind of problem-solving faculty we have found lying at the root of the sciences. It represents the 'detective' element in the researches of the humanities: trying to piece together bits of evidence, or follow up clues; but to refer to it as the 'detective' element indicates that it is not central—it is a peripheral, if important and time-consuming, activity. At the heart of the kind of understanding involved in the humanities another dimension of reason is involved, which one can perhaps call contemplative. Take the example of attempting to read, or understand, a poem. There is an element of problem-solving: the meaning of certain words no longer, perhaps, in current use, the detecting of allusions to the literary tradition to which the poem belongs—these can sometimes be 'solved' and a definitive answer produced. But having done all that, we have not finished: we have only begun—we have, as we might say, cleared the ground for an attempt to read, to understand, the poem. Here something else is involved: not a restless attempt to solve problems, to reach a kind of clarity, but rather an attempt to listen, to engage with the meaning of the poet, to hear what he has to say. We shall not do that if we misunderstand the meaning he attached to his words, or miss his allusion, but we do not necessarily hear the poet if we have simply solved all such problems. What is needed is a sympathetic listening, an engagement with the mind of the poet, and this sort of understanding has no end. There is no definitive solution: understanding is a matter of engagement, and constantly renewed engagement. *What* is understood is much more elusive in this case than what is understood when we solve a problem. It is not a matter of facts, but a matter of reality: the reality of human life, its engagement with others, its engagement with God. This resembles the notion of understanding as engagement which was introduced in the last chapter.

The distinction drawn here between two dimensions of reason, one problem-solving and the other contemplative, is obviously very close to the distinction, traditional in Western philosophy, between discursive and intuitive thought. It is also illuminated by the distinction drawn, for instance by the philosopher Gabriel Marcel, between mystery and problem:

Distinguish between the Mysterious and the Problematic. A problem is something met with which bars my passage. It is before me in its entirety. A mystery, on the other hand, is something in which I find myself caught up, and whose essence is therefore not to be before me in its entirety. It is as though in this province the distinction between *in me* and *before me* loses its meaning.

The Natural. The province of the Natural is the same as the province of the Problematic. We are tempted to turn mystery into problem. The Mysterious and Ontological are identical ...[28]

A problem is a temporary hindrance, and a proper response to it is to attempt to remove it. The mysterious is quite different: it does not so much confront me, as envelop me, draw me into itself; it is not a temporary barrier, but a permanent focus of my attention. They do overlap, though, or at least often appear to do so: for what confronts me as a puzzle, a riddle, may be either a genuine mystery, or simply a problem. Sometimes we are

---

[28] *Being and Having* (ET Fontana Library, 1965), p. 109.

presented with a problem, the solution of which precipitates us
into mystery: one recalls in this context Sir Edwyn Hoskyns's
famous exclamation, 'Can we bury ourselves in a lexicon and
arise in the presence of God?'[29] Marcel speaks of 'the transition
from problem to mystery. There is an ascending scale here; a
problem conceals a mystery in so far as it is capable of awakening
ontological overtones (the problem of survival for instance).'[30]
A problem is clarified by an attempt to dispel the darkness of
ignorance which it lays bare; we seek to explain it in terms of
something more readily understood—it is obscurantist confusion to attempt to understand *obscurum per obscurius*. With a
mystery we often find, in the words of Rückert:

> Wie oft geschieht's, dass ich ein Dunkles mir erkläre
> Durch etwas andres, das an sich noch dunkler wäre.

(How often it happens that I would explain to myself something obscure
By something else, which in itself was yet more obscure.)[31]

For it is not a matter of solving a mystery, but of participating in
it. In another passage, Marcel says a little more about his
distinction between mystery and problem:

In fact, it seems very likely that there is this essential difference
between a problem and a mystery. A problem is something which I
meet, which I find complete before me, but which I can therefore lay
siege to and reduce. But a mystery is something in which I am myself
involved, and it can therefore only be thought of as *a sphere where the
distinction between what is in me and what is before me loses its meaning and its
initial validity*. A genuine problem is subject to an appropriate technique by the exercise of which it is defined: whereas a mystery, by
definition, transcends every conceivable technique. It is, no doubt,
always possible (logically and psychologically) to degrade a mystery so
as to turn it into a problem. But this is a fundamentally vicious proceeding, whose springs might perhaps be discovered in a kind of
corruption of the intelligence.[32]

What Marcel calls the 'fundamentally vicious proceeding'
of attempting to degrade a mystery into a problem is what is

[29] *Cambridge Sermons* (London, 1938), p. 70.

[30] *Being and Having*, p. 121.

[31] Friedrich Rückert, from *Die Weisheit des Brahmanen* in *Am Abend zu lesen* (ed. G. and
T. Sartory, Freiburg, 1978), p. 34.

[32] *Being and Having*, pp. 127-8.

involved in, to use George Steiner's phrase, the 'fallacy of imitative form', which was discussed in the first chapter. For what I am suggesting is that concern for the mysterious is at the heart of the humanities, whereas at the heart of the sciences there is a concern with the problematic. That this is a contrast, and not a dichotomy, is seen in the way in which problem-solving has a place in the humanities—though the most significant kind of problem is one that, in Marcel's language, 'conceals a mystery' —and in the complementary way in which some scientists, such as Einstein, have spoken of a deepening sense of awe and wonder awakened in them, an awe and wonder in the presence of the universe, that grows through the advance of the sciences, through the growing success in solving problems. But the contrast remains, and since problem-solving can be successful, whereas contemplation of mystery cannot, there cannot be in the humanities any hope for the sort of success the sciences have known. Nor in theology: and especially not in Christian theology whose central mystery is focused in the birth of a child in a stable, and the death of a man on a cross.

In recent years several theologians have actually returned to the idea that the notion of mystery lies at the heart of Christian theology. Karl Barth in his *Church Dogmatics* sees the mystery of God's self-revelation as the heart of Christian theology. He speaks of a God who reveals himself as mystery, who makes himself known as the One who is Unknowable: 'God himself veils Himself and in the very process—which is why we should not dream of intruding into the mystery—unveils himself.'[33] This unveiling through veiling takes place in the Incarnation: so the section of the *Church Dogmatics* on the Incarnation is called 'The Mystery of Revelation'. Karl Rahner, too, speaks in very similar terms. Theology is not concerned with the elucidation of mysteries which will eventually be revealed in the beatific vision —mysteries reduced to what one might call eschatological problems. Rather, theology is concerned with the mystery of God, the mystery of the triune God who gives himself to us in love in the Incarnation of the Son. Rahner argues that there are three fundamental mysteries which lie at the heart of Christian theology: the mysteries of the Trinity, of the Incarnation, and of

[33] *Church Dogmatics*, I/1, p. 192.

the divinization of man in grace and glory. He concludes his discussion by saying, 'There are these three mysteries in Christianity, no more and no fewer, and the three mysteries affirm the same thing: that God has imparted himself to us through Jesus Christ in his Spirit as he is in himself, so that the inexpressible nameless mystery which reigns in us and over us should be in itself the immediate blessedness of the spirit which knows, and transforms itself into love.'[34]

The notion that Christian theology is to be seen as concerned with the mystery of God, the trinitarian God who loved us in Christ and calls us to participate in the mystery which he is, suggests to me that the main concern of theology is not so much to elucidate anything, as to prevent us, the Church, from dissolving the mystery that lies at the heart of the faith—dissolving it, or missing it altogether, by failing truly to engage with it. And this is what the heresies have been seen to do, and why they have been condemned: the trinitarian heresies dissolve the divine life, either by reducing it to a monadic consciousness, or by degrading it to the life of the gods; the Christological heresies blur the fact that it is in Christ that this divine life is offered to us —that it is through him and in the Spirit that we know ourselves to be loved by God himself—and do this either by qualifying the fact that God is who Jesus is, or by qualifying the fact that what Jesus is is truly a man; heresies concerning man's divinization are no less insidious, as they blur the fact that we are truly loved by God in Jesus and are called to respond to that love, and that in thus loving and being loved we are drawn into a real communion with God. But the heart of the matter is sharing in the mystery of love which God is.

I shall now try to suggest what sort of a place theology has in such a scheme of things, what sort of a study it is, what criteria it has and where it draws them from. Much of what we have discovered already has cleared the ground so that the pattern theology can and should take can be seen more clearly. We shall find that it points us along a road which is in many respects familiar—by report, at least—though not much used of late. And we shall find that it is a road, which though demanding— often much more demanding than the fashionable ways theology

---

[34] *Theological Investigations*, IV (ET London, 1966), p. 73.

has trodden recently—is also a way which leads us back to those ultimate unities that have so long eluded our grasp, unities that draw together the mind and the heart (or rather, find there a primordial unity which we have lost), unities that are nourished by love, ultimately by the love of God which is the mystery of our faith.

IV. TRADITION AND THE TACIT

SINCE the Reformation, at least, tradition has been a matter of dispute in theology: on the one hand, Catholics have been seen as using the notion of tradition to supplement Scripture, finding in it a source for those theological positions that cannot be proved from Scripture; Protestants, on the other hand, have dismissed such an idea of tradition, and have wished to keep close to the original revelation of God in Christ as witnessed to in the Scriptures. Recent scholarship, however, has shown that this simple opposition is something that developed in the course of controversy between Catholic and Protestant, and that from this point of view both those who defended it, and those who rejected it, misunderstood its nature.

One way of bringing out this misunderstanding is to notice how both sides in the Reformation and post-Reformation controversies seemed to conceive of tradition as something comparable with Scripture, either complementing it or a rival to it. Both Scripture and tradition are objectified: they are *that* which we seek to understand, there is a distance between them and us who seek to understand them. There are a good many hidden assumptions behind all this: the idea, for instance, that what is revealed is a collection of truths, so that if tradition supplements Scripture, what we mean is that in addition to the apostolic witness that was written down in the Scriptures, there are other truths which have, as it were, been whispered down the ages, and not written down. These truths are objective, independent truths, which we who seek them will, if we go about it the right way, come across and recognize. The problem of how we know at all, what it is that is taken for granted when we seek to understand God's revelation, has not been broached with any very searching intensity.

George Tavard argues[1] that this opposition of Scripture and tradition was something that arose in the later Middle Ages, and

---

[1] In his *Holy Writ or Holy Church* (London, 1959).

that it is not at all characteristic of the understanding of tradition in the Fathers or in the theology of the High Middle Ages. What I shall seek to do in this chapter is to explore some of the dimensions and implications of the understanding of tradition found in the Fathers (an understanding that continued into the Middle Ages, and was at least occasionally glimpsed by some of the writers of the Reformation period): my exploration will not be primarily historical (though I hope it will not be thought unhistorical)—such historical work has been well done by Congar[2] and others—rather I shall be concerned with the pattern of theological understanding that emerges from their attitude to tradition.

'Words, both because they are common, and do not so strongly move the fancy of man, are for the most part but slightly heard: and therefore with singular wisdom it hath been provided, that the deeds of men which are made in the presence of witnesses should pass not only with words, but also with certain sensible actions, the memory whereof is far more easy and durable than the memory of speech can be.'[3] This principle, enunciated by Hooker, of the distinction between words and deeds or actions, a distinction he uses to lay emphasis on the deeper power and significance of deeds, is a principle which not only underlies many of the crucial points of Hooker's theology (the importance of the Incarnation, and, in dependence on that, the importance of the sacraments, and indeed of liturgical worship—which is a matter not just of words but of actions—in general), but also points the way to the significance of tradition. For the central truth, or mystery, of the Christian faith is primarily not a matter of words, and therefore ultimately of ideas or concepts, but a matter of fact, or reality. The heart of the Christian mystery is the fact of God made man, God with us, in Christ; words, even his words, are secondary to the reality of what he accomplished. To be a Christian is not simply to believe something, to learn something, but to *be* something, to experience something. The role of the Church, then, is not simply as the contingent vehicle—in history—of the Christian message, but as the community, through belonging to which we come into touch with the Christian mystery.

[2] Yves M. -J. Congar, *Tradition and Traditions* (ET London, 1966), part I.
[3] Richard Hooker, *Of the Laws of Ecclesiastical Polity*, IV.i.3 (ed. J. Keble, 3rd edn. London, 1845: p. 419).

This emphasis on reality, rather than on a message or ideology, comes out in one of the passages in the Scriptures which is central to any understanding of the Christian notion of tradition:

> That which was from the beginning, which we have heard, which we have seen with our eyes, which we have looked upon, and our hands have handled, of the Word of life; (for the life was manifested, and we have seen it, and bear witness, and shew unto you that eternal life, which was with the Father, and was manifested unto us;) that which we have seen and heard declare we unto you, that ye also may have fellowship with us: and truly our fellowship is with the Father, and with his Son Jesus Christ. (I John 1:1-3).

Here the reality that John proclaims is not simply a message, but something seen and heard and handled, a genuine physical reality, and what John asks for from his readers is not belief, intellectual assent, but fellowship, a fellowship which is ultimately fellowship with the Father and the Son, fellowship with the Trinity itself. Joining a fellowship, commitment to a community, involves more than assent to its beliefs, but rather a sharing in its way of life, in its ceremonies, and customs and practices.

Now this broader understanding of what is involved in engagement with the truth, is something that has already been adumbrated in the earlier chapters of this book—in Polanyi's idea of the importance of a community and of a tradition, within which one learns to perceive and know, or in Gadamer's concept of tradition as bearing the preconceptions necessary for us to know anything at all, and of initiation into this tradition as *Bildung* or what the Greeks called *paideia*.

Werner Jaeger, in his great work *Paideia: the Ideals of Greek Culture*[4], has drawn attention to the central importance within Greek culture of the notion of *paideia*, in its dual meaning of education and culture—the process by which one is initiated into a culture. The two poles of this notion are a continuing tradition, borne by a society, and the individual who seeks to become a member of that society. Hence the importance within Greek culture of the civic virtues, justice, prudence, fortitude, and temperance. Plato's *Republic* shows how the individual is to fit

[4] ET Oxford, 1939, 1944.

himself for this society, and combines this with the idea both that life in society prepares the individual to come to knowledge of the Good, and also that such contemplation of the Good on the part of the rulers of the city-state enables them to direct the life of that society. This Greek understanding of *paideia* was taken up in the theology of the Fathers: both Irenaeus and Origen, to mention but two early examples, develop approaches to theology that revolve around the notion of *paideia*. The most fundamental reason for this, it seems to me, is that the notion of *paideia* involves taking seriously the nature of man as a social being. For the Greeks this seems to have been a kind of basic *aperçu*, for the Christians it was a consequence of their belief in God as Creator: for both it could be expressed as a belief in divine providence, fundamental for Christians, and in Plato's later philosophy, for instance, one of the basic beliefs required of those who wish to be citizens of the society he depicts in his *Laws*. Christians were driven to see the significance of all this by the challenge of Gnosticism in the second century. For Gnosticism, with its belief in the fundamentally evil character of the world and its consequent rejection of any belief in divine providence, hit at the basis of both Christianity and Hellenic culture. Such late representatives of the classical ideal as Plotinus see the heart of the error of the gnostics in their rejection of *paideia*—a natural consequence of their belief in man as an individual divine spark trapped in a hostile world. So we find Plotinus opposing, with some vehemence, the gnostics in such terms as these:

We are not told what virtue is or under what different kinds it appears ... we do not learn what constitutes it or how it is acquired, how the Soul is tended, how it is cleansed. For to say 'Look to God' is not helpful without some instruction as to what this looking imports: it might very well be said that one can 'look' and still sacrifice no pleasure, still be the slave of impulse, repeating the word 'God' but held in the grip of every passion and making no effort to master any. ... 'God' on the lips without a good conduct of life, is but a word.[5]

Christians, in opposing the gnostics, used the Greek notion of *paideia* as a way of articulating their understanding of the goodness of creation, and their understanding, consequent on this, of redemption not as something opposed to creation, as with the

---

[5] *Enneads*, II. ix.15 (tr. by S. MacKenna, rev. edn. London, 1969: pp. 147-8).

gnostics, but as the restoration of creation—a re-creation, which restored the original coherence between man and man, and man and the cosmos.

The consequence of all this was that Christians very quickly came to see that their understanding of God and his dealings with men entailed a positive evaluation of human tradition. Though there was much in the current pagan tradition that they felt they had to reject, and though such opponents of Christianity as Celsus were right when they saw in the Christians' intolerant rejection of pagan religion something that would mean the end of ancient society (hence his fundamental charge against the Christians was one of sedition), the Christian rejection of paganism was often presented (classically in Justin Martyr) as an appeal to a pristine human tradition, untainted by demonic deceit. And this involved a positive appreciation of what Jaeger, at least, presents as fundamental to Greek culture —Plato's great metaphysical vision. How such a positive concern for human tradition, an appreciation of what one might broadly call humane tradition, could be articulated within Christianity can be seen in a very significant way in Augustine's treatise *On Christian Doctrine*.

There is much dispute as to what Augustine means in this work by 'Christian doctrine' (*doctrina christiana*), but it seems to me that Marrou was right—or at least saw more deeply than others into what was involved in Augustine's enterprise—when he insisted that *doctrina* cannot be narrowly interpreted as 'doctrine' or 'teaching' (what the Church, or her accredited ministers, teaches), but means 'culture'—in short what we have been calling *paideia*.[6] For the work is concerned, as Augustine himself makes clear, with the whole enterprise of teaching and learning within the Christian community, the Catholic Church, and with all that is presupposed by this activity. This is a *Christian paideia*, and so distinct from simply pagan education, but not (as we shall see) from human culture: indeed it restores a truly human culture. This culture is learnt within the community of faith: that already distinguishes Christian *doctrina* from pagan education, for faith is faith in the unseen God, and trust in his help. And this immediately raises a question that is

---

[6] H.-I. Marrou, *Saint Augustin et la fin de la culture antique* (Paris, 4th edn. 1958), section III, especially p. 332, and Note A, pp. 549-60.

not raised where faith is not presupposed: if what is needed is faith, which is a gift of God, why does anyone need to teach anyone anything; and further, what is the point of such teaching, since what is taught will not be understood if the divine gift of faith is withheld? The latter objection is met by comparing faith with light, the light in which the truths of the Christian faith are seen. The Christian teacher points, as it were, to these truths, but, says Augustine, 'although I can lift my finger to point something out, I cannot supply the vision by means of which either this gesture or what it indicates can be seen.'[7] To the former objection, that if faith is required then there is no need of precepts and teaching, Augustine replies that those who say that 'should remember that they have learned at least the alphabet from men': the Christian faith presupposes human culture, a theme that Augustine is to develop. But further, if we are not ready to learn, because we have received the gift of faith, there is at least the danger of pride in such a refusal to submit to learning—pride in the fundamental sense of isolation of the individual—for 'charity itself, which holds men together in a knot of unity, would not have a means of infusing souls and almost mixing them together if men could teach nothing to men.'[8] Augustine makes two points here in clearing a space in which he can talk about teaching and learning within the Christian community: first, the way in which learning demands of us humility, and secondly, the fact that the Christian community is essentially a community of love, love which presupposes and perfects the togetherness of human society. Both these points will be developed later, both in relation to human tradition and also in relation to the tradition of the Church.

Augustine begins Book I of *On Christian Doctrine* by making a distinction beween things and signs, *res* and *signa*: signs point beyond themselves to things, but things are what they are, though only discerned and understood through signs. The word *res* has, in fact, a resonance in Latin which is obscured by the English word 'thing' or 'reality'. In his work on Vergil (from which we have already quoted) Theodor Haecker, in commenting on the words from the *Aeneid,* 'sunt lacrimae rerum',

---

[7] *On Christian Doctrine: prologue,* 3 (tr. by D. W. Robertson, New York, 1958: p. 4).
[8] Ibid., *prologue,* 6 (Robertson, p. 6).

draws attention to the way in which the word *res* is used in Latin to designate reality in a way both comprehensive and concrete. So the State is called *res publica*; history is just *res* and a historian a 'writer of things', *rerum scriptor*; the greatest philosophical poem in Latin is significantly entitled *De rerum natura*; Rome as the capital of the Empire is *caput rerum, domina rerum.* Haecker illuminates the significance of the word *res* in Latin by introducing the idea of a heart-word (*Herzwort*) of a language:

The invisible, individual spirit of a people is finally revealed in all its external, visible business, but most clearly in the living body of its language. And from each such body of a language we hear words which sound from the heart, which betray to us where this individual heart is most inclined, what is its greatest care, what its grief, its longing, its passion, its joy and its pleasure is. Because they are the most inward to the body of a language, such heart-words are understandably the most difficult to translate. At best they are to be left, as and where they are, at any rate if there is to be any complete understanding. In order to understand *these* words, one must already have gained access to the whole language.[9]

He suggests that we can find such 'heart-words' in *logos* in Greek, in *raison* in French, in 'sense' in English, in *Wesen* in German: and in Latin *res* is such a heart-word. So it is the word Augustine uses in his *On Christian Doctrine* to designate things, the reality disclosed to us by signs. To treat of things is to treat of what is fundamental, and this Augustine proposes to do for the rest of Book I.

Book I turns out to be a treatise on love. When we are dealing with things as they are, we are at the level of *love*: the moral primacy of love reflects an ontological primacy. Augustine develops his doctrine of love by using the distinction between *frui* and *uti*—enjoying and using. To enjoy something is to cleave to it for its own sake; to use something is to love it for the sake of something else. God alone is to be loved for his own sake; people are to be loved in him because with them we can share our delight in God; things are to be used. Here we have a doctrine of *ordered love,* and for Augustine our love can only be properly ordered when we submit in humility to learn from the Incarnate Word of God. To imagine that we can order our love and cleave

---

[9] *Vergil, Vater des Abendlandes,* (Munich, 5th edn. 1947), p. 110.

to God alone in our own strength would be pride: and it is such pride that Augustine found in the endeavours after self-culture (a merely humanly administered *paideia*) among the Neo-platonists.

The heart of the matter, then, is love, and it is this love that the Scriptures are to teach us. How Scripture teaches us this, is what Augustine goes on to discuss in Books II and III. Scripture teaches us through *signs*, and just as Book I was about things, so Books II and III are about signs, *signa*, and how they are to be interpreted. First Augustine distinguishes between natural signs (*signa naturalia*) and conventional signs (*signa data*). He does this to dispose of *signa naturalia* (smoke as a sign of fire, a contorted expression on the face of a man as a sign of pain), for though they are an important way of communicating, they provide no basis for any developed form of human communication. It is by means of *signa data* that we communicate with one another, and the most important form of such signs is words (for though anything that can be understood can be explained through words, words themselves cannot be explained exhaustively in terms of any other conventional signs). Words can be made permanent through letters and writing. Augustine then makes the important point that *signa data* depend for their efficacy on consent among human beings, and that it is just such consent among human beings that makes possible human society. Words cannot be regarded as natural signs (which would not require such human consent), for even though we often try to make words correspond with what they signify (Augustine knows as well as more recent investigators into the origins of language about the part played by onomatopoeia in the formation of words), 'since one thing may resemble another in a great variety of ways, signs are not valid among men except by common consent'. Augustine's whole discussion of language and signs, with the important place it gives to the notion of consent, emphasizes the way in which the whole enterprise of human understanding is something that cannot be understood in a purely individualistic manner, but on the contrary depends upon and grows out of a shared tradition, a common sense. And in fact for the most part Augustine means by this shared tradition, this common sense, a shared *human* tradition, a common *human* sense. Only occasionally does he tighten this sense of shared tradition to mean the shared tradition of the Church: rather he emphasizes how the human enterprise of knowing and coming to understanding involves the common human tradition of those who speak the same language and interpret their experiences in the same way.

Chapter 7 of Book II gives a summary account of how we are to approach and use Scripture so as to come to the knowledge of God. Augustine presents this approach as a ladder with seven steps. We begin with the fear of God, and quickly pass to the next step, which is piety, *pietas*. In this way our pride is cut down and piety enables us to approach Scripture in a receptive spirit: we are approaching Scripture willing to learn, we are accepting its claim to have something to teach us. The third step is *scientia*, knowledge. This comprises all the knowledge we need in order to *understand* the Scriptures: it involves knowledge of languages, knowledge of various kinds presupposed by the Scriptures (natural history, a certain amount of history, logic, numbers, music, and so on), the knowledge required to establish accurate texts. It also comprises a knowledge of the Scriptures themselves: we are to read the Scriptures, and commit a great deal of them to memory, for it is in the Scriptures as a whole that we find the voice of God speaking to us. What Augustine has in mind here is not any sort of method, but rather a deep familiarity with the language and content of the Scriptures. Such a reading of the Scriptures, as Congar has said of the Patristic approach to the reading of the Scriptures as a whole, 'is sapiential in form and founded on a double conviction: first, everything is the work of the Word or Wisdom of God; second, God does not manifest and communicate himself in words alone, and so ultimately in ideas, but in realities.'[10] As a result of all this, the student discerns from Scripture that he is enmeshed in the love of this world, a love very remote from the kind of love of God and of our neighbour that the Scriptures commend. The next step is fortitude, by which the student avoids falling into despair and turns to a love of the eternal. The fifth step is the counsel of mercy, which urges us on to love of our neighbour and thereby leads to a purging of the mind. On the sixth step the soul is filled with love of his enemy, and here 'he cleanses that eye through which God

---

[10] *Tradition and Traditions*, p. 67.

can be seen'. The top step is *sapientia,* wisdom. 'The fear of the
Lord is the beginning of wisdom': that sentence from Proverbs is
drawn out by Augustine into a ladder by means of which we
ascend through Scripture to wisdom, knowledge of God not in
the sense of knowledge about God, but rather of communion
with him.

What Augustine offers us here is reminiscent of similar ladders
of ascent to God which we can find elsewhere in Augustine, and
in the Christian tradition both before and after him, and indeed
more widely. They are ways in which the soul prepares itself for
knowledge of, union with, God; they consist of purification of
the soul by the practice of the virtues. In the Christian tradition
such 'ladders' reach back to Plato and the Platonic tradition,
where the virtues are seen as restoring a man to harmony with
himself, and thus enabling him to accomplish that for which he
was made: the vision of God. We can then join together—or
rather see the deeper connection between—Augustine's emphasis on human tradition, as underlying any human enterprise
of knowing and coming to understanding, and his adumbration
of an approach to the Scriptures as a way of spiritual ascent to
the knowledge of God; for they both spring out of an understanding of Christian *paideia* that is continuous with, and a
development of, the understanding of *paideia* developed among
the Greeks, and in particular given classical expression in the
works of Plato.

But the specifically *Christian* understanding of tradition goes a
great deal futher than this, though we shall see that something of
the pattern that has emerged already remains, but is deepened
and developed. Let us begin by quoting a few significant passages from the writings of the early Fathers. First a passage from
Clement of Rome: 'The apostles were taught the Gospel for our
sake by the Lord Jesus Christ, and Jesus the Christ was sent
from God. Christ therefore was from God, and the apostles from
Christ; in both ways then things were brought about in an
ordered way by the will of God.'[11] This recalls the passage
quoted earlier from the first epistle of St. John, and recalls too
such passages from St. John's Gospel as 'As my Father hath sent
me, even so send I you' (20:21), 'As thou hast sent me into the

---

[11] *I Clement,* 42.1-2 (*Die Apostolischen Väter,* Funk-Bihlmeyer, Tübingen, 1970: p. 57).

world, even so have I sent them into the world' (17:18), 'And the glory which thou gavest me I have given them; that they may be one, even as we are one: I in them, and thou in me, that they may be made perfect in one; and that the world may know that thou hast sent me, and hast loved them, as thou hast loved me' (17:22-3). Jesus is the One sent from God the Father; the apostles are those whom he has sent into the world. Whereas tradition understood in a human sense is perhaps the continuity of man's search for the truth, and whatever progress there is in such a search, tradition in the sense of the tradition of the Church is the continuity of the divine sending, the divine mission, which the Church has received from her Lord and which she pursues in the world. The Scriptural passages we have quoted, and the passage from *I Clement*, speak of the Church's sending as echoing the Father's sending of his Son into the world, but to understand its full significance we need to recall other passages from St. John's Gospel: 'Receive ye the Holy Ghost' (20:22, the very next verse after the first one we quoted), 'But when the Comforter is come, whom I will send unto you from the Father, even the Spirit of truth, which proceedeth from the Father, he shall testify of me: and ye also shall bear witness, because ye have been with me from the beginning' (15:26-7), 'But the Comforter, which is the Holy Ghost, whom the Father will send in my name, he shall teach you all things, and bring all things to your remembrance, whatsoever I have said unto you' (14:26). The Church's sending is in the power of the Spirit: the heart of the Church's tradition, Holy Tradition, is the life of the Holy Trinity, in which the Church participates through the Holy Spirit, the fellowship which is 'with the Father, and with his Son Jesus Christ'.

A passage from St. Irenaeus takes us somewhat further:

The true knowledge is the teaching of the apostles; and the ancient order of the Church found throughout the world; and the character of the Body of Christ according to the succession of bishops, to whom the Apostles committed (*tradiderunt*) that Church which is in each place, and which has come even to us, preserved without any writings by the fullest exposition [i.e. the rule of truth] which admits of neither increase nor diminution; and reading of the Scriptures without any falsification and their legitimate and careful exposition, avoiding danger and blasphemy; and the special gift of love, which is more precious than knowledge, and more glorious than prophecy, surpassing all other charisms.[12]

Here we have more detail as to how the tradition is passed on throughout the history of the Church. Irenaeus speaks of the character of the Church which is preserved through the succession of bishops: by this he means not just the articles of faith handed down by the apostolic succession of bishops, but the whole character of the Christian community, its rites, its ceremonies, its practices, and its life. The final point he makes about the 'special gift of love' underlines the fact that for Irenaeus the tradition of the Church is not, like the traditions to which the gnostics appealed, simply some message, truth, or ideology, but a life, something lived.

In the passage quoted Irenaeus alludes to the rule of truth (as he usually calls it; others call it the rule of faith, *regula fidei*, which is how it is usually known). Early on in his *Adversus Haereses*, he says that 'one who possesses undeviatingly the rule of truth, which he received in baptism, and knows the names of the Scriptures, and the sayings, and the parables, will not recognize the blasphemous suggestions that they [the gnostics] put forward',[13] and goes on in the next chapter to explain the rule of truth thus:

For the Church which is disseminated throughout the whole world, right to the ends of the earth, received from the apostles and their disciples the faith in one God the Father Almighty, maker of heaven and earth, the seas and all that is in them; and in one Christ Jesus, the Son of God, who was incarnate for our salvation; and in the Holy Spirit who prophesied through the prophets about the economies, and the comings, and the birth from the Virgin, and the passion, and the resurrection from the dead, and the ascension into heaven of the body of the beloved Christ Jesus our Lord, and his coming from heaven in glory of the Father to sum up all things ...[14]

The rule of truth, then, is the faith, the fundamentals of Christian belief. It is the basis of the creed, which developed later on in the history of the Church.[15] This is the tradition which has

[12] *Adversus Haereses*, IV. xxxiii.8 (ed. W. W. Harvey, Cambridge, 1857, vol. II, pp. 262-3).

[13] Ibid. I.ix.4 (Harvey, I, pp. 87-8).

[14] Ibid. I.x.1 (Harvey, I, pp. 90-1).

[15] See J. N. D. Kelly, *Early Christian Creeds* (London, 3rd edn. 1972) and R. P. C. Hanson, *Tradition in the Early Church* (London, 1962).

been handed down from the apostles and is received in baptism: the fact that it is *received* is almost as important as what is received —tradition is not something we make up, but something we accept. So Congar remarks illuminatingly at the beginning of the systematic section of his book on tradition:

Tradition, taken here in its broadest meaning, is an example, the chief example, of the quite general law of man's dependence on, and obligation towards, his fellows. Elementary analysis of the concept of tradition, as a matter of transmission or delivery, shows moreover that *two* persons are implied, one to transmit and one to receive. This structure of human interdependence or brotherly mediation is a very important feature, of the human condition in the first place, and so also of the Christian condition. We belong to, and are part of, a world. Fecundation by another, recourse to another in order to fulfil oneself— this is a general law of life, at least in corporeal beings. We can bring about our own death, but we cannot give ourselves life. In the closed world of living creatures, species even live on one another, and the balance of the whole system is assured by the cooperation of the individual parts—'it is a vast web, a seamless garment.' In the normal course of events we receive our faith from another; we cannot baptize ourselves. Thus, it is normal for persons to depend on one another in order to achieve their supernatural destiny. In our sharing in the divine life through another's mediation we may see a reflection of the divine life itself, which is the self-giving of one Person to another.[16]

Further dimensions of the notion of ecclesiastical tradition come out in the remarks St. Basil makes in the course of his work *On the Holy Spirit.* Here he makes a distinction between *kerygma* and *dogma*: 'We have both dogmas and proclamations (*kerygmata*) preserved in the Church, proclamations in the written teaching, and dogmas which we have received from the tradition of the apostles and given to us in secret.'[17] But Basil is not appealing to some secret, 'whispered' tradition that has come down from the apostles: the sort of thing of which Irenaeus denied the very existence a couple of centuries earlier. The examples Basil gives of such unwritten traditions are all liturgical practices: the sign of the cross, prayer towards the East, the epiclesis at the Eucharist, and indeed most of the rest of the Eucharistic prayer, the blessing of water in baptism, of oil, and

[16] *Tradition and Traditions*, pp. 240-1.
[17] *On the Holy Spirit*, XXVII.66 (ed. C. F. H. Johnston, Oxford, 1892: pp. 127-8).

so on. The secret tradition is not a message, but a practice, and the significance of such practice. We come back to the fact that Christianity is not a body of doctrine that can be specified in advance, but a way of life and all that this implies. Tradition is, as it were, the tacit dimension of the life of the Christian: what is proclaimed (for Basil, the *kerygmata*) is only part of it, and not really the most important part. This comes out if we realize the significance of Basil's appeal to tradition here. For Basil's appeal to tradition is his ultimate defence of the divinity of the Holy Spirit: a defence which, significantly, he cannot express wholly in words. He never in this work says explicitly that the Spirit is of one substance—*homoousios*—with the Father and the Son, for to write it down would be to make it public, make it a *kerygma* (and his reticence here is shared by the Creed accepted at the Second Ecumenical Council of Constantinople in 381). But the truths of *theologia*—in the strict Cappadocian sense, the doctrine of God as he is in himself; the doctrine of the Trinity, therefore, which we attain when we recognize the divinity of the Holy Spirit—these truths are *dogmata*.[18] That means they are not truths that can be proclaimed, they are not 'objective' truths which could be appraised and understood outside the bosom of the Church: rather they are part of the Church's reflection on the mystery of her life with God.

This becomes clearer, perhaps, when we look at the arguments Basil uses in *On the Holy Spirit* to prove that the Spirit is God. These arguments all revolve around the Christian's experience of the life of grace, or as Basil would more naturally put it, life in the Spirit. The life of the Christian is a participation in the life of God, and this cannot take place without the Spirit. The work of sanctification is the work of the Spirit:

As for the union of the Spirit with the soul, he manifests his presence not by spatial approach (for how can one speak of space when thinking of the corporeal and the Incorporeal?), but by the exclusion of passions which assail the soul from the love of the flesh and separate it from intimacy with God. To be cleansed therefore from this shame contracted by wickedness, and return to the beauty of one's nature, and receive through purity one's pristine form in the royal image, thus is the only way one can approach the Paraclete. And he, like the sun

18 Ibid. XX.51 (p. 102).

reflected in a clear eye, shows you in himself the image of the Invisible;
in the blessed contemplation of the Image, you will see the ineffable
beauty of the Archetype.[19]

Basil then goes on to say that as a result souls become spiritual—
diaphanous to the Spirit—and become themselves sources of
spiritual illumination for other souls. What this means Basil
sums up as 'prevision of the future, understanding of mysteries,
comprehension of hidden things, the distribution of spiritual
gifts, a heavenly life, fellowship with the angels in their praise,
unceasing joy, rest in God, likeness to God, and the summit of
their desires: they become God.'[20] For Basil all this is only
possible in the Spirit. One of his ways of expressing this is to
speak of the Spirit as intelligible light (*phos noeton*) in which the
soul becomes mind or *nous*. As *nous* the soul can contemplate: in
the Holy Spirit, intelligible light, it is enabled to contemplate the
Image of the Archetype, the Son of the Father. Even the angels
can see nothing apart from the Holy Spirit, the light of the
intelligible realm: for 'as in the night, if you remove the light
from your house, your eyes will be blind, their powers inert, all
you value indistinct, so that, through ignorance, gold and iron
appear alike. So in the intelligible order it is impossible, apart
from the Spirit, to lead a life conformed to the law ...'.[21] The
same idea is being expressed when he says:

Since through an illuminating power we reach forth to the beauty of
the Image of the Invisible God, and through that come to the surpassing vision of the Archetype, this cannot take place apart from the
presence of the Spirit of knowledge, who gives in himself to those who
love the vision of truth the power to behold the Image, not doing this
as an external act, but receiving us into Himself for this knowledge ...
as it is written, In thy light shall we see light, that is, in the illumination
of the Spirit we shall see the true light, that lightens every man coming
into the world.[22]

As the Spirit makes possible our participation in the divine
life, so he himself must be divine. But this can hardly be stated,
for the premiss is only available to those who participate in the
divine life. For others there is nothing to appeal to. And even for
those who do know this participation in the divine life, it is

[19] Ibid. IX.23 (p. 53).   [20] Ibid. (pp. 53-4).
[21] Ibid. XVI.38 (p. 82).   [22] Ibid. XVIII.47 (pp. 94-5).

difficult to state anything objectively and clearly about the Spirit, for he is not what we perceive, but that in virtue of which we perceive anything at all. We might put it like this: that it is difficult to say anything about the Spirit, for we are only in a position to say anything at all, when we are in that very place where the Spirit is. Here 'Truth is Subjectivity'.

What this seems to suggest is that ultimately the tradition of the Church *is* the Spirit, that what is passed on from age to age in the bosom of the Church is the Spirit, making us sons in the Son, enabling us to call on the Father, and thus share in the communion of the Trinity. Modern commentators have seen this implied in the words St. John uses to record the death of Jesus: 'and gave up the ghost' (*paredoken to pneuma*—and passed on, or handed over, the Spirit: 19:30). Hoskyns comments:

> But it is very strange language. If it be assumed that the author intends his readers to suppose that the Beloved Disciple and Mary the Mother of Jesus remain standing beneath the cross, the words *He bowed his head* suggest that He bowed His Head towards them, and the words *He handed over the Spirit* are also directed to the faithful believers who stand below. This is no fantastic exegesis, since *vv.* 28-30 record the solemn fulfilment of vii.37-9. The thirst of the believers is assuaged by the rivers of living water which flow from the belly of the Lord, the author having already noted that this referred to the giving of the Spirit.[23]

This exegesis is supported by Lightfoot[24] and is sympathetically considered by Barrett[25], though it is interesting to note that it appears to be quite unknown in the Fathers.[26]

Understood like this, tradition is not another source of doctrine, or whatever, alongside Scripture, but another way of speaking of the inner life of the Church, that life in which the individual Christian is perfected in the image of God in which he was created. Speaking of it as tradition brings out the fact that it is received, that it is participated in, that it is more than the grasp that the individual has of his faith. To quote Congar again: 'Tradition involves not merely a recollection, but also a deepen-

[23] E. C. Hoskyns and F. N. Davey, *The Fourth Gospel* (London, 1940), p. 633.

[24] R. H. Lightfoot, *St. John's Gospel* (Oxford, 1956), p. 319.

[25] C. K. Barrett, *The Gospel according to St. John* (London, 2nd rev. edn. 1978), p. 554.

[26] M. F. Wiles, *The Spiritual Gospel* (Cambridge, 1960), p. 67.

ing of insight; it is preserved, not merely in the mind, but also in the 'heart', which meditates lovingly on what it holds fast (cf. Luke 2:19, 57); it involves not merely a fidelity of memory, but also a fidelity of living, vital adherence.'[27]

Here we see the importance of liturgy for the realization, and continuity, of tradition, and thus why it is that when Basil appeals to a tradition that goes beyond Scripture, he appeals to the liturgy. For it is, most fundamentally, in the celebration of the liturgy, and especially in the celebration of the Eucharist, that we realize and celebrate the mystery of Christ, that we share in and come to know the Son's offering himself to the Father in love and obedience. For the heart of the Christian faith is not something simply conceptual: it is a fact, or even better, an action—the action, the movement, of the Son sent into the world for our sakes to draw us back to the Father. And it is this movement that the liturgy, with its dramatic structure, echoes and repeats. As Dom Gregory Dix has finely said: 'There is but *one* coming, in the incarnation, in the Spirit, in the eucharist and in the judgement. And that is the 'coming' of 'One like unto the Son of Man' (who is 'the people of the saints of the Most High', i.e., Christ and the church) *to the Father*. This is the end and meaning of human history, the bringing of man, the creature of time, to the Ancient of Days, in eternity. The same eternal fact can touch the process of history at more than one point …'.[28] Liturgy is not something we 'make up', nor is it something that can be simply 'understood': it is something we participate in, not just as minds, but with all that we are—body and soul. Hence the importance in the liturgy of gestures and movement, of the sequence of the seasons, through which time itself is sanctified. The liturgy unfolds the varied significance of the mystery of Christ, and the fact that it cannot all be explained, the fact that much that we do, we do simply because we have always done it, conveys a rich sense of the unfathomableness of the Christian mystery. Basil undertakes to explain, or give a provisional explanation of, some of the ceremonies he has cited as belonging to the unwritten, the secret, tacit tradition of the Church. 'It is for this reason that we all look to the East at the time of prayer, though few of us know that we thus look to our

---

[27] *Tradition and Traditions*, p. 15.
[28] *The Shape of Liturgy*, (Westminster, 1945), pp. 262-3.

ancient homeland, Paradise, which God planted in Eden towards the East.' He gives several other explanations of the various practices of the Church, but concludes, 'Even a whole day would not suffice for an explanation of the unwritten mysteries of the Church.'

The danger of attempting to reduce the liturgy to what can be understood in simple conceptual terms is one that has beset the West since at least the time of the Reformation, and it is a marked feature of much modern liturgical reform. It is a danger it has been one of the purposes of this chapter to warn against. What can be articulated, what can be understood, is only a part, if an important part. The life in which we share as we commit ourselves to the tradition of the Church goes much deeper. At the Reformation the English Church preserved a liturgy, preserved a sense of continuity with the past, and it is worth while in this context to recall Hooker's defence of the principle of the liturgy:

The end which is aimed at in setting down the outward form of all religious actions is the edification of the Church. Now men are edified, when either their understanding is taught somewhat whereof in such actions it behoveth all men to consider, or when their hearts are moved with any affection suitable thereunto; when their minds are in any sort stirred up unto that reverence, devotion, attention, and due regard, which in those cases seemeth requisite. Because therefore unto this purpose not only speech but sundry sensible means besides have always been thought necessary, and especially those means which being object to the eye, the liveliest and most apprehensive sense of all other, have in that respect seemed the fittest to make a deep and a strong impression: for hence have risen not only a number of prayers, readings, questionings, exhortings, but even of visible signs also; which being used in performance of holy actions, are undoubtedly most effectual to open such matter, as men when they know and remember carefully, must needs be a great deal the better informed to what effect such duties serve. We must not think but that there is some ground of reason even in nature, whereby it cometh to pass that no nation under heaven either doth or ever did suffer public actions which are of weight, whether they be civil and temporal or else spiritual and sacred, to pass without some visible solemnity: the very strangeness whereof and difference from that which is common, doth cause popular eyes to observe and mark the same ...

The things which so long experience of all ages hath confirmed and made profitable, let not us presume to condemn as follies and toys, because we sometimes know not the cause and reason of them. A wit disposed to scorn whatsoever it doth not conceive, might ask wherefore Abraham should say to his servant, 'Put thy hand under my thigh and swear:' was it not sufficient for his servant to shew the religion of an oath by naming the Lord God of heaven and earth, unless that strange ceremony were added? ...[29]

Hooker gives several other examples and concludes by quoting from Denys the Areopagite's *Ecclesiastical Hierarchy*: 'the sensible things which religion hath hallowed, are resemblances framed according to things spiritually understood, whereunto they serve as a hand to lead, and a way to direct.'

The importance of liturgy, then, for tradition is that by the very fact of its being performed, of its being the doing of something that others have done before us, of its being a matter of significant actions that suggest meaning rather than define it, it introduces us into a context, a realm of values, in which the significance of tradition can be seen. By the fact that it goes beyond speech, it impresses on us the importance of the inarticulate: and it is not without significance that inarticulateness about what is deeply important is characteristic of the child, whom we have to be like if we are to enter the kingdom of heaven.

This stress on inarticulateness can be developed in another way. In an essay called 'Tradition and Traditions', Vladimir Lossky suggested that one fruitful way of considering tradition is to think of it as silence. If Scripture is the word, the voice, the utterance, then tradition is, in contrast, silence. Lossky quotes from St. Ignatius of Antioch: 'He who possesses in truth the word of Jesus can hear even its silence', and remarks that the significance of this passage for the Patristic understanding of tradition has not apparently been previously noted. Lossky develops this idea by speaking of a 'margin of silence' which belongs to the words of Scripture and which cannot be picked up by the ears of those who are outside. He links this up with something Basil says in his *On the Holy Spirit:* 'There is also a form of silence, namely the obscurity used by the Scriptures, which is intended in order to make it difficult to gain understanding of the teachings, for the profit of readers.' This idea of an obscurity

---

[29] *Ecclesiastical Polity,* IV.i.3 (pp. 418-19).

inherent in the Scriptures, an obscurity that is penetrated only within the Church, within the tradition of the Church, is something we shall explore in more detail in the next chapter when we consider the notion of allegory.

Lossky also develops this idea from Ignatius by speaking of tradition as the *unique mode* of receiving the truth of revelation:

> We say specifically *unique mode* and not *uniform form,* for to Tradition in its pure notion there belongs nothing formal. It does not impose on human consciousness formal guarantees of the truths of faith, but gives access to the discovery of their inner evidence. It is not the content of Revelation, but the light that reveals it; it is not the word, but the living breath which makes the words heard at the same time as the silence from which it came (cf. Ignatius of Antioch, Magnesians 8:2); it is not the Truth, but a communication of the Spirit of Truth, outside which the Truth cannot be received. 'No-one can say "Jesus is Lord" except by the Holy Spirit' (I Cor. 12:3). The pure notion of Tradition can then be defined by saying that it is the life of the Holy Spirit in the Church, communicating to each member of the Body of Christ the faculty of hearing, of receiving, of knowing the Truth in the Light which belongs to it, and not according to the natural light of human reason.[30]

This recalls ideas I have already developed from Basil's consideration of tradition and the Holy Spirit. But Ignatius' words point us further in a slightly different direction. 'He who possesses in truth the word of Jesus can hear even its silence': the word for 'silence' here is *hesychia*, which is silence or *stillness*. Ignatius is talking about the stillness necessary for us to hear the words of Jesus: a stillness which implies both receptiveness and presence. We come back to a point I have repeatedly emphasized: that Jesus did not simply communicate a message. The apostles were those who had been *with* him, not simply those who knew what he said. Indeed there is something about the words of Jesus, even in the Fourth Gospel, that makes us feel that what is being communicated is deeper than mere words, deeper than any mere message. Hort puts it well: 'The power of the Life that dwelt in Christ comes forth in His words. There are hardly any precepts among them, nothing could be less like the edicts of a law-giver. Almost all are calm affirmations of truth, often

---

[30] *In the Image and Likeness of God* (London, 1975), pp. 151-2.

sounding like repetition and like vagueness. Yet while the terms elude all efforts at definition the sense of each as a whole is seen to be unutterably precise as we study it.'[31] To hear Jesus, and not just his words, we have to stand within the tradition of the Church; we have to put our trust in those to whom our Lord entrusted' his mission, his sending. Part of the stillness that is needed for us to hear the words of Jesus is a sense of presence, and it is this that tradition conveys. We become Christians by becoming members of the Church, by *trusting* our forefathers in the faith. If we cannot trust the Church to have understood Jesus, then we have lost Jesus: and the resources of modern scholarship will not help us to find him.

Stillness, silence: which I suggested means both presence and receptiveness. Receptiveness, and attentiveness: and these are qualities deepened and realized in prayer. When Ignatius lays emphasis on the importance of 'hearing its silence', at least part of what he means is the importance of a kind of docile receptiveness, in contrast with the spirit which listens in order to put what is heard to its own uses. And this is something we need to cultivate, we need to learn. Again the liturgy provides an important context for this, as the words are repeated and brought again and again to our consciousness, and thus enabled to penetrate beneath our surface minds to our very heart. 'The Gospel in the heart': this is one of the ways in which Congar sums up the notion of tradition. 'The Gospel written in men's hearts goes far beyond the written text, despite the fact that what is written is itself, in a sense, inexhaustible. The Fathers were well aware of this.'[32] 'Written in the heart' meaning dwelt on, pondered on— of which Mary's 'pondering in her heart' is the profoundest example—and expressed not just in the attaining of some conceptual enlightenment, but in what we do. 'Not to *hear* the word', as St. Gregory the Great puts it, 'is not to put it into practice in one's life.' Or one could simply continue our quotation from St. Ignatius: 'He who possesses in truth the word of Jesus can hear even its silence, that he may be perfect, that he may do through what he speaks and know through that of which he is silent.'

---

[31] F. J. A. Hort, *The Way, The Truth, The Life* (London, 1897), p. 205.
[32] *Tradition and Traditions,* p. 348.

The notion of tradition as silence is also witnessed to in another way in the Church's life. If we think of Jesus' communicating by his presence and by his words, what we are pointing to is expressed by the importance and power of the *living voice*. Within the Church we learn the Christian faith from particular individuals, it is not something we can learn from books. Similarly we learn how to pray from others. Here we meet the notion of the spiritual director as an organ of the tradition: Clement of Alexandria's *gnostic*, the spiritual fathers of the Eastern tradition, and especially of the desert tradition, the *startsi* of the Russian tradition. Here what is important is the relation of the disciple to his master, to the voice of his master. Men visited a Desert Father to 'ask for a word'. These words can be, and were, collected: but the heart of the experience was the word of a holy man spoken to a particular person in a particular context. It is interesting to note that this tradition is primarily concerned with love, and prayer, what one might call 'undogmatic' matters, and yet it was representatives of this tradition of seemingly undogmatic piety who played an important role in the defence of the Church dogmatic tradition in the fourth century and thereafter. The living voice of the master, the one who through prayer and self-discipline has come to know, that is, come to communion with the heart of the faith, has immediacy and directness, and incarnates the fundamental experience of encounter with the living Lord. Jerome remarked that 'the effect of the living voice has some strange and hidden power; it has greater resonance when coming direct from the mouth of the master to the ear of the disciple.'[33]

If we see tradition as the life of the Holy Spirit in the Church, then we must also see it as something that brings us into the freedom that the Spirit confers, the 'boldness' (*parresia*) that enables us to stand in the divine presence and speak with simplicity of what is there made known. It is in some such way that we should see the Fathers: as those who spoke with such *parresia* that their words have the immediacy of direct witness. From such a point of view the age of the Fathers is not past, though certainly the archetypal 'Patristic' voice is something we recognize in those who formed the fundamental dogmatic tradition of the Church.

---

[33] *Epistle* 53, quoted ibid., p. 368.

Congar puts it thus: 'When we see the Fathers in this way, as those who have formed the milieu of the Church's historical growth ... we find that they are unanimous, we are at the heart of the real consensus. We have seen that Tradition is for a Christian almost what the educational milieu is for man in general; the child needs to form its own conclusions in a milieu which provides him with security; it is fundamentally the role of the consensus of the Fathers to provide such an element in the Church.'[34] Such openness to the Spirit, issuing in freedom and *parresia*, is not won without effort: the Fathers were saints, they were men of prayer. Again to quote Congar: 'Their work was blended with prayer, fasting, penitential exercises and the life of divine union. This gives to many of their writings a tone which puts them among "the writings of an eye-witness about the country of his birth".'[35] And so we find Hort saying: 'the moment we study the greater theologians who have done more than reflect or even systematize current beliefs, we find the harmony of contemporary assumptions broken, and we often find also these isolated but not isolating voices to reflect the inarticulate feelings of the simply devout who are not theologians.'[36]

We make contact again with an inarticulate living of the mystery, the tacit dimension, which is the heart of tradition, and from which theology must spring if it is to be faithful to the truth it is seeking to express. For the truth that lies at the heart of theology is not something there to be discovered, but something, or rather someone, to whom we must surrender. The mystery of faith is not ultimately something that invites our questioning, but something that questions us.

[34] Ibid., p. 400.
[35] Ibid., p. 449, quoting Ivan Kireevsky.
[36] *The Way, the Truth, The Life*, p. 186.

V.   RETURN TO ALLEGORY

IF we look back to the Fathers, and the tradition, for inspiration as to the nature of theology, there is one thing we meet which must be paused over and discussed in some detail: and that is their use of allegory in interpreting the Scriptures. We can see already that for them it was not a superfluous, stylistic habit, something we can fairly easily lop off from the trunk of Patristic theology. Rather it is bound up with their whole understanding of tradition as the tacit dimension of the Christian life: allegory is a way of entering the 'margin of silence' that surrounds the articulate message of the Scriptures, it is a way of glimpsing the living depths of tradition from the perspective of the letter of the Scriptures. Of course the question of allegory in the Fathers is complex (and often rendered unduly complicated by our own embarrassment about allegory): but whatever *language* the Fathers use to describe their exegetical practice (and there is no great consistency here), they all interpret Scripture in a way we would call allegorical, and *allegoria* is the usual word the Latin Fathers use from the fourth century onwards to characterize the deeper meaning they are seeking in the Scriptures. Some of the Fathers, it is true, attack what they call allegory and its use; but what they are attacking are the results (particularly the results that Origen came up with) and not a method. The beginning of Augustine's literal commentary on Genesis is the *locus classicus* of such an attack; but Augustine himself was no stranger to allegorical interpretation of the Scriptures. Even the Antiochene Fathers admit of a deeper spiritual meaning (which they call not *allegoria* but the 'contemplative' meaning—*kata theorian*), and if the greatest of them, Theodore of Mopsuestia, is shy in his use of it, this shyness is interpreted as a limitation, a 'disappointment', by a recent scholar who has himself no enthusiasm for the Fathers' love of allegory.[1]

But it is Patristic allegorization that sticks in the gullet of modern theology, and not just 'modern theology' in some limited sense: at all levels this allegorization is something

---

[1] M. F. Wiles, *The Spiritual Gospel* (Cambridge, 1960), p. 159.

deplored. To give an example almost at random: in a recent
issue of the *Oxford Diocesan Magazine* David Peck felt obliged to
warn readers of some of the limitations of Patristic theology, in
a review of a book giving an account of the understanding of
Christian initiation in the early centuries. 'The reader', he says,
'will also be made aware of some difficulties. The instruction
these candidates received was peppered with "spiritual" interpretation of scripture, in other words, "typology" (the raven
which flew from the ark was sin and so on *ad infinitum*). Such
interpretation seems to us quite remote and the theological
implications dubious.'[2] One could not complain: David Peck is
fulfilling the reviewer's function admirably in pointing out to the
unwary reader the doubts and hesitations of modern theology
over the enterprise of 'allegory'. Other general characteristics
which mark off Patristic from modern theology we find much
less distressing: the background of Platonism, the cosmology
implied (three-tier universe and so on). All that, we can in a way
take: we can interpret it, excuse it, seek to understand it—but
not allegory. There seems to be a fundamental distaste for, or
even revulsion against, the whole business of allegory.

Why is this? Basically, I think because we feel that there is
something *dishonest* about allegory. If you interpret a text by
allegorizing it, you seem to be saying that it means something
which it patently does not. It is irrelevant, arbitrary: by allegory,
it is said, you can make any text mean anything you like. Behind
this, perhaps, lies a feeling that there is something relatively
unproblematic about the meaning of a literary passage: roughly,
the meaning is what the author of the passage meant when he
wrote it. This may, of course, be difficult to get at: it is often
difficult to understand what someone is trying to say, and all
such difficulties can easily be magnified when we are dealing not
with a person we can interrogate, but with a piece of literature
written by someone long dead, in historical circumstances we
can only reconstruct with more or less probability. It may well be
difficult to get at the meaning of a literary passage, it may be
impossible to be sure that we have arrived at this meaning: but
the idea that the text means what the author meant it to mean—
the idea, almost, that the meaning of a text is a past historical

[2] December 1980, p. 19.

event—gives us a sense that the meaning of a text is something objective, something unproblematic. The way of allegory often seems to ignore all this (often, not always, despite the general opinion: for Augustine, in developing his theory of the interpretation of Scripture in *On Christian Doctrine,* takes it for granted that the meaning of a text is what the author intended, and so sees allegorical meanings as part of what the author intended; the same is true, it seems to me, *mutatis mutandis,* of Austin Farrer). By now it will be apparent that the general feeling that lies behind such a resistance to allegory—the sense of the unproblematic nature of the meaning of a literary passage—is not well founded: the ideas of Gadamer already expounded show that it is full of unexamined idealization.

Within *theology* this abhorrence of allegory because of the way it seems to ignore the objective meaning of Scripture is reinforced by the legacy (itself often unexamined) of the Protestant principle of *sola scriptura.* Scripture is objective truth, the objective truth of God's revelation. Allegory, then, seems to be a way of evading the address of God to man in the Scriptures, a way of adulterating the purity of divine revelation with human opinions and conjecture. Allegory, from such a point of view, is fundamentally faithless, irreligious. Luther (in his tract against the Louvain theologian Latomus, for example) was fundamentally and deeply opposed to allegory and to the concomitant idea of the multiple senses of Scripture, for Scripture is the One Word of God which must be heard as addressing man unequivocally with a unique, single voice (not that this prevented Luther from having resort to allegory on other occasions). Keble is not far wrong when he says in the first paragraph of his tract *On the Mysticism attributed to the Early Fathers of the Church* (*Tract* 89 of the *Tracts for the Times,* no less remarkable, though less notorious, than *Tract* 90—the 'mysticism' Keble refers to includes as its major constituent the idea that Scripture has a 'mystical sense', that is, the use of allegory): 'During the struggle of the Reformation, men had felt instinctively, if they did not clearly see, that the Fathers were against them, so far as they had begun to rationalize, whether in ecclesiastical practice, or in theological inquiry'[3]—and nowhere more so than in the way Scripture was

---

[3] London, 2nd edn. 1868, p. 1.

utilized, utilized in a way which made the traditional use of allegory something that seemed profane and irreligious. But the principle of *sola scriptura* suggests that the truth of the Christian religion is contained in Scripture, and that the work of the theologian and exegete is to extract this truth by rightly interpreting Scripture. We remember that the Fathers preferred to work out their theology in the context of the interpretation of Scripture (and conveniently forget *how* they set about this task), we remember that the medieval theologian was one learned in the interpretation of the *sacra pagina*: it seems, then, that the task of the theologian is to find a way of unlocking the objective truth of the Scriptures, the objective meaning contained in the Scriptures.

It is curious to realize how this whole approach (an approach which, I am arguing, is not in the least traditional—unless one regards what stems from the Reformation as traditional) has been both scuppered and reinforced by the growth of the method of historical criticism. Reinforced: because the method of theological criticism does seem to be a way, a procedure, of discovering the objective meaning of a text, the intention of the author who wrote the text. I have already discussed the way in which the historical-critical method seems to offer itself as the scientific method appropriate to literary studies. It has what appears to be the great merit of *objectivity*: both in the sense that the object of study seems clear—it is what the author of a text had in mind when he wrote it—and in the sense that the truth discovered is independent of the one who discovers it. Link this with the principle of *sola scriptura* and one seems to have a method which promises the very truth of God revealed in the Scriptures. And methods have a certain fascination: they seem to promise so much, they give one the sense of discovering things, of making progress. There are not many biblical scholars who point out as candidly as did a recent Bampton Lecturer (A. E. Harvey) that to speak of modern *discoveries* in relation to the New Testament is somewhat of a misnomer: new interpretations, maybe, but the evidence is what it always was, and that has long been available.

But whatever this method *promises*, what it delivers seems less exciting. The method promises to give us the pearl of the truth of God hidden in the field of Scripture. But if with one hand the method seems to reinforce the principle of *sola scriptura*, with the

other it leads to disappointment: for it produces no *pearl* at all,
not even a little one. What it delivers is often thought to be
slight and uncertain. We can respond to this state of affairs in a
number of ways. We can, with the liberals—or at least with the
more honest and straightforward of the liberals—frankly say
that theology is not essentially the interpretation of Scripture: we
drop the idea that *sacra doctrina* is drawn from *sacra pagina*. So
Professor Wiles holds that to speak of 'all doctrine being in the
end exegesis' is 'untenable'; it is, he says, 'either plainly false or
else … a very misleading way of expressing a possible position.'[4]
Or we can try various conservative ploys. We can boldly maintain that the historical-critical method, if applied to the Scriptures cautiously, does indeed yield the desired pearl. We deplore
the scepticism and extremism of the radical critics (usually
German, though there are notable German representatives of
this conservative approach). But we can never be sure that we
are not making things too easy for ourselves, that our caution in
our use of the historical-critical method is not essentially arbitrary and dictated by conclusions we know we want to reach
anyway. This seems to be part of Professor Barr's criticism of the
fundamentalists: but it is a criticism that could easily be generalized. Another conservative ploy is to keep the historical-
critical method as our key to the truth, but to widen its scope by
dropping the principle of *sola scriptura* (or attacking it, never
having held it anyway). If the results that the historical-critical
method yields when applied to Scripture are too meagre, maybe
we shall do better if we include the creeds, the Councils, and
the Fathers. But it is not clear that the ground is then all that
much more secure: for the Fathers, and creeds, and Councils
claim to be interpreting Scripture. How can one accept their
results if one does not accept their methods? It might be possible
to argue that if they had had the benefit of the historical-critical
method they would still have ended up at Chalcedon. But on the
one hand such a claim seems a bit far-fetched, and on the other it
is so unhistorical a notion as to be scarcely coherent. It might be
better to go back to the liberal position and say that theology is
not essentially about the interpretation of Scripture at all, and
that therefore the Fathers' theology is of interest in itself and is

---

[4] *Working Papers in Doctrine* (London, 1976), p. 96.

not (much) affected by their (mistaken) belief that all they were doing was drawing out the meaning of the Scriptures.

The presupposition that lies behind all this—a presupposition either defended (more or less desperately) or finally relinquished —is the principle of *sola scriptura,* understood as meaning that Scripture is a quarry from which we can extract the truth of God's revelation: that allied to the more recent notion that the tool to use in extracting meaning from literary texts is the method of historical criticism. We have an alliance between the Reformation and the Enlightenment: not something that inspires confidence. But as will be clear from our considerations so far, both the principle and the method are questionable.

The principle of *sola scriptura* actually leads one away from the traditional devotion to Scripture as the Word of God which we find *par excellence* in the Fathers. Scripture is being understood as an arsenal and not as a treasury (to use the contrast drawn by Paul Claudel in his *Du sens figuré de l'Écriture*[5]). And such an understanding leads to a false and misleading notion of the nature of Christianity as a biblical religion. If the bible is seen as a quarry from which truth is to be extracted, then the truth thus extracted—the truth of Christianity—is naturally seen as 'biblical'. Other quarries produce other 'truths', similarly labelled—'Platonic', 'Canaanite', or whatever. It is then felt to be important not to mix up the different kinds of truth—for they are different rocks from different quarries—and it is felt that some have thus erred. But as Henri de Lubac protests in his *Exégèse Médiévale*:

Christianity is not, properly speaking, a 'religion of the Book': it is a religion of the word (*Parole*)—but not uniquely nor principally of the word in written form. It is a religion of the Word (*Verbe*)—'not of a word, written and mute, but of a Word living and incarnate' (to quote St. Bernard). The Word of God is here and now, amongst us, 'which we have looked upon, and our hands have handled': the Word 'living and active', unique and personal, uniting and crystallizing all the words which bear it witness. Christianity is not 'the biblical religion': it is the religion of Jesus Christ.[6]

And in those words de Lubac echoes the cry of St. Ignatius of

[5] Published in *Oeuvres complètes,* vol. 21, *Commentaires et exégèses* (Paris, 1963), p. 11.
[6] *Exégèse Médiévale,* II/1 (Paris, 1961), pp. 196-7.

Antioch: 'For me the archives are Jesus Christ, and the inviol-
able archives his cross and death and his resurrection and faith
in Him.'[7] The heart of Christianity is the mystery of Christ, and
the Scriptures are important as they unfold to us that mystery,
and not in and for themselves.

So much—briefly—for the principle of *sola scriptura,* Scripture
as an arsenal rather than a treasury. But our modern understanding of the Bible joins this principle with another: the
principle of the *method.* I have already criticized this in a rather
different context, so it will be sufficient to recall the main lines of
this criticism and see its bearing here. The points in Gadamer's
criticism of the Romantic hermeneutic of the historical-critical
method that are particularly relevant here are his criticism of the
notion of an 'original meaning' of a text, and the way in which he
restores the notion of tradition to its place in our endeavour to
understand the writings of the past. The notion of the 'original
meaning' is attacked as being a false idealization underlying the
Romantic method of interpretation. As we saw, the real aim of
Romantic hermeneutics is not so much an understanding of the
literary work as an understanding of the author: we are seeking
to divine the author's original intention by painstakingly
reconstructing his original context. This, as Gadamer point out,
ignores the fact that I have my own historical situation and
cannot leap out of it into someone else's. There is something
Promethean about Schleiermacher's and Dilthey's Romantic
ideal of understanding an author 'better than he understood
himself'. We are seeking to relive the author's original creative
inspiration, with the hope of doing so with greater understanding than the author himself, as the author's whole life has
now been lived and is (to some extent) accessible to us. Gadamer,
rather, wants to see understanding as engagement with what a
writer wrote, and thus (and only thus) engagement with him.
Understanding is the result of genuine engagement: it is less a
result with an objective content than an event in the life of the
one seeking to understand. Understanding a writer of the past is,
in Hegel's phrase which I have already quoted, a 'thinking
mediation with present life'. So Gadamer can say things like:
'What is fixed in writing has detached itself from the contin-

---

[7] *Ep. Philad.* VIII.2 (Funk-Bihlmeyer, p. 104).

gency of its origin and made itself free for new relationships. Normative concepts such as the author's meaning or the original reader's understanding represent in fact only an empty space that is filled from time to time in understanding';[8] 'not occasionally only, but always, the meaning of a text goes beyond its author'—this does not mean that our understanding is superior to that of the author: 'it is enough to say that we have understood in a different way, if we understand at all.'[9]

What Gadamer says here recalls certain ideas about interpretation associated with the name of T. S. Eliot. In his essay 'The Frontiers of Criticism', Eliot suggests that 'there is, in all great poetry, something which must remain unaccountable however complete might be our knowledge of the poet, and that that is what matters most. When the poem has been made, something new has happened, something that cannot be wholly explained by *anything that went before*. That, I believe, is what we mean by "creation".'[10] Eliot goes on in the essay to mention certain dangers he sees in any *method* of interpreting poetry (actually he has in mind the method he associates with the influence of I. A. Richards, but his points are of general import). There is the danger, he says, 'of assuming that there must be just one interpretation of the poem as a whole, that must be right'. Certainly there are some things one can get right (or wrong)— matters of fact, historical allusions, and so on—but, as Eliot puts it, 'as for the meaning of the poem as a whole, it is not exhausted by any explanation, for the meaning is what the poem means to different sensitive readers.'[11] The meaning is not some 'objective content', rather we might say meaning takes place when there is communication through the poem between the poet and his reader, when there is engagement between the poet and the reader. Another danger Eliot draws attention to is 'that of assuming that the interpretation of a poem, if valid, is necessarily an account of what the author consciously or unconsciously was trying to do. For the tendency is so general, to believe that we understand a poem when we have identified its origins and traced the process to which the poet submitted his

---

[8] *Truth and Method*, p. 357.
[9] Ibid., p. 264.
[10] *On Poetry and Poets* (London, 1957), p. 112.
[11] Ibid., p. 113.

materials, that we may easily believe the converse—that any explanation of the poem is also an account of how it was written.'[12]

The poet has created something new in his poem (Latin *poema* from the Greek *poiema*, 'something made'): to understand a poem is to understand the new thing that it is, not to have access to the process by which it came into being. 'Der Dichter stellt seine Schöpfung in der Welt hinaus,' said Goethe (the poet exposes his creation to the world). The roles of the poet and the interpreter are different, and the poet is not necessarily the best, and certainly not a privileged, interpreter of his work. 'It is not for the poet to be his own interpreter and analyse his work minutely in everyday prose; if he did so, he would cease to be a poet. The poet exposes his creation to the world; it is the task of the reader, of the aesthete, of the critic to investigate what he willed with his creation.'[13]

Eliot reflected further on this in his essay 'Virgil and the Christian World', which introduces other ideas that are pertinent to our considerations here. Apropos of the fourth Eclogue, which since the time of Lactantius has been taken by Christians as a prophecy of the birth of Christ, Eliot distinguishes between the conscious intention of a poet and what may legitimately be seen in his work, and uses the notion of 'inspiration' to bridge the gap.

That Virgil was himself consciously concerned only with domestic affairs or with Roman politics I feel sure: I think that he would have been very much astonished by the career which his fourth Eclogue was to have. If a prophet were by definition a man who understood the full meaning of what he was saying, this would be for me the end of the matter. But if the word 'inspiration' is to have any meaning, it must mean just this, that the speaker or writer is uttering something which he does not wholly understand—or which he may even misinterpret when the inspiration has departed from him. This is certainly true of poetic inspiration: and there is more obvious reason for admiring Isaiah as a poet than for claiming Virgil as a prophet. A poet may believe that he is expressing only his private experience; his lines may be for him only a means of talking about himself without giving himself

---

[12] Ibid., pp. 113-14.
[13] Conversation with Heinrich Luden, August 1806; quoted in Eudo C. Mason, *Goethe's Faust: Its Genesis and Purpose* (London, 1967), p. 35: I owe this reference to my colleague, F. J. Lamport.

away; yet for his readers what he has written may come to be the expression both of their own secret feelings and of the exultation and despair of a generation. He need not know what his poetry will come to mean to others; and a prophet need not understand the meaning of his prophetic utterance.[14]

Scholars and historians are concerned with establishing Virgil's intentions (though we have seen from Gadamer that this may not be as unproblematic as it might seem), with what Virgil *thought* he was doing. Eliot accepts that, but adds, 'if there is such a thing as inspiration—and we do go on using the word—then it is something which escapes historical research.'[15] We recall that Christians too use the notion of 'inspiration' in relation to the Scriptures, and though we may be none too clear what this notion involves, we can see that it could be held to imply that the Scriptures, as 'inspired', have the ability to speak to changed times and changed circumstances, have therefore a voice that escapes the limitations of the particular circumstances to which they were originally addressed. We might indeed say that to speak of the Scriptures as inspired means that the Church has found them, throughout the ages, to speak to her with a continually fresh authority.

The other relevant point in Gadamer's critique of the historical-critical method is his reconsideration of the place of tradition. As he points out, the method of historical criticism stemming from the Enlightenment and the Romantics attempts to break the thread of tradition. The interpreter of a literary work tries to approach it without presuppositions, he tries to stand outside the literary tradition to which he belongs. Tradition is seen as something that confuses and falsifies. Clearly we have here a transfer to the realm of the humanities of something experienced in the realm of the sciences. For there it was only as the hold of traditional ways of understanding natural phenomena was broken and science learnt to rely on an experimental method which sought results (as far as possible) independent of the observer, that science made any progress. But the natural order of physical objects and the moral order of intelligent beings are not at all the same. It is not as a physical

---

[14] *On Poetry and Poets,* pp. 122-3.
[15] Ibid., p. 123.

object that we investigate the natural order, whereas it *is* as an
intelligent being that we inhabit the moral order and seek to
understand it. The moral order is transparent to us in a way the
natural order is not (a point made by both Vico and Dilthey),
and the medium of that transparency is tradition, tradition
formed by language and custom. What lies between us and the
men of the past is what Gadamer calls 'the infinite intermediary
of tradition', which is 'not a yawning abyss, but is filled with the
continuity of custom and tradition, in the light of which all that
is handed down presents itself to us'.[16] Gadamer speaks of
tradition as being 'constantly an element of freedom and of
history itself' in the sense that it is not something dead and fixed,
which would endure like granite in the natural order: 'even the
most genuine and solid tradition does not persist by nature
because of the inertia of what once existed. It needs to be
affirmed, embraced and cultivated ...'.[17] Here too one could
draw parallels beween Gadamer and Eliot, but this is not the
place to elaborate them.[18]

The effect of all this is to put the act of understanding in a
wider context than the historical-critical method suggests or
allows, and in this wider context we are in a better position to
appreciate the traditional way of understanding the Scriptures
as it is found *par excellence* in the Fathers, a way of understanding
that sees not one but many senses of Scripture, and draws these
senses out by the use of allegory. To begin with, what is, I
suspect, the root of our unease about allegory is taken away: that
is, the idea that a text of Scripture has an 'original meaning'
which the method of allegory ignores or evades. Instead of
rejecting the way of allegory outright, what we have to ask is
whether this way focuses our attention on the text of Scripture
in such a way that we are more able to hear what it has to say to
us, more alert, more sensitive, to the voice of God in the Scriptures. I shall argue that, properly understood, it does just that.
But the other notion I have underlined in Gadamer's critique of
the method of historical criticism points us on the way forward
more obviously: this is the idea that in interpreting a piece of

[16] *Truth and Method,* p. 264.
[17] Ibid., p. 250.
[18] For Eliot on tradition see, especially, his article 'Tradition and the Individual
Talent', in *Selected Essays,* (London, 3rd end. 1951), pp. 13-22.

writing it is not a matter of my attempting to reconstruct the original historical context in which it was written and thus to divine what was originally meant in an act of imagination, but rather a matter of my listening to what was once written, listening across a historical gulf which is not empty, however, but filled with the tradition that brings this piece of writing to me, and brings me not only that piece of writing but pre-conceptions and prejudices that enable me to pick up the resonances of the images and arguments used in whatever it is I am seeking to understand. Gadamer argues this in a primarily secular context: he is mainly concerned with the interpretation of the classical writers, when he comes himself to the practical task of interpretation—but the *terms* in which he defines his task are terms he has drawn, ultimately, from theology. The very notion of tradition, as we have seen, is a Christian (and Jewish) notion—for Plato, for example, *paradosis* had a primarily negative significance—and the pattern Gadamer develops is a pattern in which the Christian theologian will find much that is familiar: indeed within Christian theology it has, or has had, a depth and significance beyond anything Gadamer dreams of. For it must be said, in passing, that Gadamer himself would probably not make much of the sort of development I am going to suggest for his ideas. A pupil of both Bultmann and Heidegger at Marburg, he has not, it seems to me, any very live awareness of tradition in a theological sense. He would probably reject it on the usual Protestant grounds, though the sort of things he says about tradition contain many hints for a Catholic defence of the value of tradition.

It was seen in the last chapter that tradition is that by which we receive Scripture and the context within which we interpret it. What unites us with the writers of the Scriptures is the life of the Church from their day to ours. It was in the life of the Church that the Scriptures emerged, but in the Church that they were recognized as Scripture, and in the Church that they are read as Scripture—as opposed to being read as ancient Hebrew litera-ture and the writings of one of the new religions that infested the world of late Roman Hellenism. There is a symbiosis between Scripture and tradition: Scripture feeding tradition and tradi-tion providing the kind of receptiveness in which Scripture can be read as Scripture.

This might be developed in a number of ways. Let me suggest two: one an illustration, one more an expansion. We might consider the way in which the idea of the complementarity of Scripture and tradition makes ready sense of what we know of the formation of the Old Testament. For here too historical criticism has had the odd effect of both advancing our understanding and denying us that understanding. The notion of 'original meaning' is here very complicated: do we mean what was intended by the one who first uttered a prophetic oracle, for example, or the one who first wrote it down and regarded it as a significant oracle, or the one—or more likely the many—who edited it and gave it its place in the context of the whole prophetic book as we have it? Or take the psalms, particularly their use in Christian worship: what is the meaning of these poems that we recite, and continue to recite after three thousand years or so? Is it what the original writer intended, or what whoever it was who introduced the psalm into the worship of the Temple thought, or what? Clearly too restrictive an understanding of the meaning of a psalm will make nonsense of the recitation of the psalms and deny the basis of the spiritual experience of generations of Christians. And what about those who collected the books together and formed them into a canon? And which canon anyway? It makes a good deal of difference, it seems to me, whether the Prophets come at the end of the Old Testament or somewhere in the middle of the Hebrew Scriptures. The tendency of the historical-critical method has been to concentrate on originality and regard what is not original as secondary: but if we see here a process of inspired utterance and reflection on—comment on—inspired utterance within the tradition, itself regarded as inspired, then we have a more complicated, but, I suggest, truer picture. The formation of the Hebrew Scriptures is an object lesson in the kind of complementarity of Scripture and tradition—or inspired utterance and tradition—that I have outlined. The art of understanding is more complicated, and richer, than an attempt to isolate the earliest fragments and to seek to understand them in a conjectured 'original' context: we hear the voice and the echoes and re-echoes, and it is as we hear that harmony that we come to understanding. As I see it, it is this perception that underlies the notion of 'canon criticism', associated particularly perhaps with the name of Brevard Childs.[19]

But here is another illustration, of a rather different kind. I have spoken of tradition 'echoing' the Scriptures, which suggests the idea of tradition as some kind of echo-chamber, or better, let us say, a cathedral. Imagine attending high mass in a cathedral—it had better be a medieval French cathedral, about twenty years ago. The action of the mass takes place; we see the gestures and the movements, we hear the chanting and the singing. The meaning of what we are participating in we absorb in what is potentially almost an infinity of ways. Images contained in the words may draw our attention to something in the cathedral—a statue, an arch, a picture in the glass. Things seen, things heard, may recall other things seen and heard, in the same place, on another occasion. We may be struck with analogies between what we can hear and what we can see. Some of this—not likely very much of this on any one occasion: that would mean we were distracted—kindles our devotion, and focuses our heart on the *mysterium Christi* being done before us. A potentially infinite variety of shape and form and association, all drawn from the mystery of the Eucharist, all drawing us back to the mystery of the Eucharist. That is for me some sort of an image of the way Scripture finds, or is found to possess, an infinity of richness in the bosom of the Church's tradition.

The appeal of the way of allegory—or more directly here, the realization of the multiple sense of Scripture—comes from this recognition of the *mira profunditas* of the Sacred Scriptures. It is this *mira profunditas* which Newman celebrates in a famous passage from his *Essay on Development*:

It is in point to notice also the structure and style of Scripture, a structure so unsystematic and various, and a style so figurative and indirect, that no one would presume at first sight to say what is in it and what is not. It cannot, as it were, be mapped, or its contents catalogued; but after all our diligence, to the end of our lives and to the end of the Church, it must be an unexplored and unsubdued land, with heights and valleys, forests and streams, on the right and left of our

---

[19] See, e.g., his *Introduction to the Old Testament as Scripture* (Philadelphia, 1979). Also in this context mention should be made of the works of A. G. Herbert (especially *The Throne of David* (London, 1941) and *The Authority of the Old Testament* (London, 1947)), which raised many of these questions years ago and have been strangely neglected since.

path and close about us, full of concealed wonders and choice trea-
sures.[20]

Mira profunditas: a sense of the depth and richness of Scripture,
a richness derived from the mystery to which it is the introduction, of which it is the unfolding. A depth, a complexity, a
difficulty. But this is not the way we ought to be going. To make
Scripture difficult, to make the gospel a mystery, a puzzle—
is not this the way of the gnostics?

Perhaps we should pause here and consider what we mean by
'difficulty'. In a fairly recent article[21] George Steiner has discussed this and proposed, at least provisionally, four different
types of difficulty we may find in reading literature, four types he
distinguishes by calling them 'contingent', 'modal', 'tactical',
and 'ontological'. 'Contingent' difficulty is very straightforward: it is the difficulty we find when we encounter words we
do not understand, or allusions we do not recognize. What we
lack here is knowledge, and when we have acquired that knowledge the difficulty vanishes. 'Modal' difficulty is rather
different: here it is not a matter of needing to know things,
needing to 'do our homework'—rather it is that even when we
have done our homework we find the poem, or whatever it is,
difficult to place: it does not speak to us, it does not summon us
and we cannot find an appropriate response. Here the difficulty
lies not exactly in the poem we seek to understand, but in ourselves: there does not seem to be within ourselves that which can
respond. A further type of difficulty Steiner identifies as
'tactical': this has its source in the will of the writer, or in his
failure to achieve adequately what he is setting out to perform. It
is an obscurity we can 'place' by reference to the writer: he may
be trying to escape the interference of the censor (Nadezhda
Gorodetsky finds here the key to understanding the deeper
meaning of many Russian writers of the nineteenth century[22]),
he may not wish to reveal precise personal circumstances, or
whatever. Beyond these three types of difficulty Steiner speaks of
a further kind which he calls 'ontological' difficulty: 'difficulties

---

[20] *An Essay on the Development of Doctrine* (rev. edn. London, 1891), Part I, chap. 11,
sect. I, para. 6 (14): p. 71.
[21] 'On Difficulty', in *On Difficulty and other Essays* (Oxford, 1978), pp. 18-47.
[22] *The Humiliated Christ in Modern Russian Thought* (London, 1938).

of this category cannot be looked up [as with contingent diffi-
culties]; they cannot be resolved by genuine readjustment or
artifice of sensibility [as with modal difficulties]; they are not
about an intentional technique of retardation and creative
uncertainty [as with tactical difficulties].'[23] It is a difficulty
which seems to question the very nature of poetry itself and to
demand of the reader a radical reorientation as to what meaning
is at all. It is not trying to say anything we might anticipate:
rather it is trying to call into question our very anticipations.
Examples Steiner gives of such ontological difficulty are to be
found in the poetry of Mallarmé and Paul Celan. Steiner's
discussion of difficulty recalls Marcel's distinction between
problem and mystery discussed earlier: contingent difficulty is
clearly a kind of problem, and there is something of the problematic in modal and tactical difficulty—there is the possibility of
solution; but ontological difficulty is something very like the
mysterious—there is no answer, only engagement.

I do not know that there is any very direct transition to be
made from such considerations of difficulty to the 'difficulty' in
Scriptures to which allegory is a response. But it does seem to me
that this response sees that difficulty not as contingent (in
Steiner's terms), but as deeper, and therefore as demanding of
the reader not just more information, but some kind of reorientation. It is not a way of obfuscation, as it would be if allegory
were a device for solving 'contingent' difficulties: rather allegory
is a way of holding us before the mystery which is the ultimate
'difficulty' of the Scriptures—a difficulty, a mystery, which
challenges us to revise our understanding of what might be
meant by meaning; a difficulty, a mystery, which calls on us for
a response of *metanoia*, change of mental perspective, repent-
ance. H.-I. Marrou saw something of this when, in his generous
Retraction to his *Saint Augustin et la fin de la culture antique*, he with-
drew some of the hard things he had said about Augustine's
learning (or lack of it) and his resort to allegory: 'If Holy Scripture is not only the sacred history of sinful humanity and of the
economy of salvation, a deposit of oracles revealing to the Church
both truths, properly natural, which men run the risk of misunderstanding, and also illumination of mysteries inaccessible

---

[23] *On Difficulty*, p. 41.

to humanity, if it is *also* that forest of symbols suggesting to us under the appearance of figures the same truths of faith, we must have the courage to conclude that God Himself is *also* a poet.'[24] And he goes on to say that 'St. Augustine invites us to rediscover in the Scriptures a Mallarmean conception of poetry.'[25] A 'difficult' play of symbols and metaphors 'to purify the dialect of the tribe' and to recall us to the simplicities we have lost in our sophistication. For what one discovers in allegory, according to Augustine—and he speaks for all the Fathers in this—is the faith of the simple believer. The use of allegory in relation to Scripture, seen from such a point of view, is not an attempt to solve problems, contingent difficulties, but a means of ensuring that we do not evade the fundamental 'ontological difficulty' which opens us to the ultimate mystery of Christ contained in the Scriptures. The difficulty in Scripture arises from the depth of its signification, and forces us to find a point of stability, or is rather a warning that we have yet to find it. It is the difficulty of not being sufficiently at home in the tradition, not having an unerring instinct as to what resonates and what merely makes a noise. And what we need here is no method— there is none—but rather erudition, learning, experience: the experience of living close to the heart of tradition, of being able to hear His stillness, to quote St. Ignatius—a familiarity with the response that Scripture has inspired in the Church throughout its life.

It is important to realize this: that the traditional doctrine of the multiple sense of Scripture, with its use of allegory, is essentially an attempt to respond to the *mira profunditas* of Scripture, seen as the indispensable witness to the mystery of Christ. This is the heart of the use of allegory. Now, this is not at all the impression one gets from the more popular introductions to the Fathers' use of allegory (or indeed from some of the more scholarly discussions). On the contrary, allegory is presented as a device for solving problems ('contingent difficulties') presented by the sacred text. Much is made of the way Origen several times remarks that inconsistencies in the historical narrative presented in the Scriptures are there to alert us to the fact that the

---

[24] Paris, 4th edn. 1958, pp. 648-9.
[25] Ibid., p. 649.

true meaning of Scripture is not to be found at the level of the historical narrative (or literal meaning) at all. Allegory is what Origen uses to paper over the cracks in a supposedly inspired and infallible text. But R. L. P. Milburn is probably nearer the truth when he says of Origen that 'he aimed not so much to depreciate the events of Biblical history as to proclaim that their significance was richer and fuller than an uncomprehending analysis would allow,'[26] and summarizes Origen's own account of his way of proceeding thus: 'Origen declares the whole Scriptural record to be God's symphony, wherein the inexpert listener may think he perceives jarring notes whilst the man whose ear has been well trained realizes the fitness and grace with which the varied notes are worked up into one harmonious composition.'[27] We are not concerned with a technique for solving problems but with an art for discerning mystery. Not that allegory may not be abused and used as a mere problem-solver, nor that this was not something the Fathers and their successors were aware of and warned against, as this passage from Hugh of St. Victor bears witness:

The words are plain and clear enough. You understand each separate clause: *seven women shall take hold of one man* and so on. But perhaps you cannot understand what it means as a whole. You do not know what the prophet wishes to say, whether he is promising good or threatening disaster. And, so it happens, you think that a passage whose literal meaning you do not grasp should be understood only in a spiritual sense. So you say that the *seven women* are the seven gifts of the Holy Spirit, who *shall take hold of one man,* that is Christ ... who alone 'takes away their reproach' that they may find in him a refuge ...

Lo! you have expounded spiritually and you do not understand what it means literally. But the prophet could mean something literally too by these words.[28]

Of course, the Fathers often did resort to allegory to solve problems presented by the text of Scripture that were beyond their grasp. In my defence of allegory I am not at all attempting to defend that, or to deny that there are many problems in the Scriptures that can be satisfactorily solved by the methods of

[26] *Early Christian Interpretation of History* (London, 1954), p. 42.

[27] Ibid., p. 50, summarizing Origen in *Philokalia*, vi.2.

[28] *Didasc.* VI.iv.807-8, quoted in Beryl Smalley, *The Study of the Bible in the Middle Ages* (Oxford, 1952), p. 94.

historical criticism (in so far as they are valid). The discovery of different strands in the Pentateuch does helpfully clear up many problems presented by the text as we have it. And having been solved they are just that—solved, disposed of. But the mystery to which allegory seeks to hold us is very different: it is enduring, it is never 'solved'. But it can be ignored, or missed. And if we are to think of allegory as a way of focusing on the mystery to which the Scriptures bear witness, we should ask of allegory whether it actually succeeds in holding before us that mystery, or better, in holding us before that mystery, so that we are questioned by it, and not allowed to ignore it, or miss it.

So far we have seen how the path might be open for considering allegory as a way of interpreting Scripture, and further it has been suggested in what *context* we might consider it as such a way: not as a technique for solving problems, but as a means of focusing on the mystery that lies at the heart of Scripture and lends to Scripture a sense of *mira profunditas*. But what is it anyway? How does allegory operate? Even granted that it is not a method or a technique, but, as Keble put it, a 'style of interpretation' detectable 'by something in its air and tone; something not the less real, because it may be to us indescribable in words',[29] it must still have a certain structure, and be subject to some principles: and indeed it does.

Enormous light has been shed on this by Père Henri de Lubac in his great work (too little read, to judge by the paucity of reference to it in the *Cambridge History of the Bible,* for example), *Exégèse Médiévale,*[30] which explores the traditional doctrine of the four senses of Scripture. Despite its title it is as much concerned with Patristic exegesis as medieval, for it is de Lubac's contention that the approach to Scripture found in the Fathers continued to be the fundamental approach throughout the Middle Ages, at least until the time of St. Thomas Aquinas and St. Bonaventure (*pace* the theories of Miss Beryl Smalley[31]), and after sharing in the decay of late medieval theology, was rediscovered by Erasmus, among others, and had indeed been preserved amongst the mystical writers. As the title suggests, though, most of his discussion concerns the Latin West.

[29] *On the Mysticism attributed to the Early Fathers of the Church,* p. 40.
[30] *Exégèse Médiévale: Les quatre sens de l'Ecriture,* I/1 & 2 (Paris, 1959), II/1 (1961), II/2 (1964).
[31] Referred to above, p. 5.

When we think of the doctrine of the senses of Scripture we commonly think of them as consisting of three or four: the literal, first, then the moral or tropological, the mystical or allegorical, and finally the anagogical. Reduced to three, they become the literal, the moral, and the mystical, and a famous passage in Origen's *De Principiis* (influential through its inclusion in the collection called the *Philocalia*, compiled from Origen's works by St. Basil the Great and St. Gregory Nazianzen) speaks of these three senses of Scripture as corresponding to the threefold nature of man—body, soul, and spirit. The body of Scripture is the literal sense, the soul of Scripture the moral sense, and the spirit the mystical or allegorical sense. If one starts from this point, one quickly gets the idea that the moral and mystical senses are other ways of using Scripture which more or less ignore the literal sense. The moral sense seems pretty innocuous: the Bible is a 'good book' and the idea that it contains examples we should follow seems reasonable, if not pushed too far. (But it is fairly arbitrary: not all biblical examples are good examples—we are in fact using a moral standard we already have in lighting on particular examples as improving.) The allegorical sense seems to be an attempt to make Scripture say something it manifestly does not say: the text of Scripture becomes a peg on which doctrinal disquisitions can be hung. Understood like this, the literal sense seems to be downgraded, the moral sense arbitrary but probably pretty innocuous, the allegorical sense really quite frivolous.

The very prominence, though, of the text from *De Principiis* may well mislead us into exaggerating its significance. It is well known that Origen does not systematically work through the three senses in his commentaries and homilies: more often he works with a simple distinction between literal and allegorical, letter and spirit, shadow and reality, old and new, what is simply believed and what is food for contemplation. Commonly little significance is seen in this: it is a truncation of the threefold sense developed in *De Principiis*, and Origen maybe was not very interested in the moral sense, regarding it, perhaps, as fairly obvious.

One of the first things de Lubac investigates in his *Exégèse Médiévale* is something that might seem at first sight trivial, but which turns out to be of enormous significance: and that is the *order* of the sense of Scripture.

> Littera gesta docet, quid credas allegoria
> Moralis quid agas, quo tendas anagogia.

(The literal sense teaches what happened, allegory what you are to believe, the moral sense what you are to do, anagogy where you are going.) That couplet, cited thus by Nicholas of Lyra, is perhaps the most familiar form of the doggerel mnemonics about the senses of Scripture (there are, in fact, many such). It is echoed by many passages in the Fathers (the later Fathers, that is) and the medieval writers which summarize the traditional teaching. But note the order: first the literal, second the allegorical, third the moral, fourth the anagogical. De Lubac shows that this order is the most common, the most traditional. Another order, found less often though also traditional, switches the allegorical and moral, so that we get: literal, moral, allegorical, anagogical. This latter order is easily seen to be a development of the threefold sense of Scripture put forward by Origen in *De Principiis* in analogy with the threefold constitution of man: allegorical and anagogical are just two different ways of developing the mystical sense. This latter order, stemming from Origen, is used by Ambrose and Jerome and developed by Cassian and Eucherius; the former order, which places the allegorical sense before the moral, can be traced back to Augustine and Gregory the Great. And it is this order that is not only the commonest and most traditional, but also the most fundamental and profound. For it is not just a list of senses, but an order or a movement: we move from history to allegory, and within allegory we perceive first the dogmatic dimensions of the Christian mystery, then the response it calls for on our part (the moral sense), and then finally we are given a glimpse of the fruition of the mystery which calls us on (the anagogical sense). The other order, which places the moral sense before the allegorical, is simply a list—a summary of the different dimensions in which Scripture can be understood. The fundamental order, which places allegory before the moral sense, makes the moral sense depend on the allegorical sense: it is our response to what is disclosed by the allegorical sense. In this case, as de Lubac puts it, 'there is expounded an ascesis and a mysticism which can be characterized as Christological, ecclesial and sacramental: it is a veritable history of the spiritual life, founded on dogma.'[32] De Lubac points out that the organic connection of the allegorical, moral, and anagogical senses means that we have fundamentally a twofold division here between the literal and the allegorical, and (with reason) traces this twofold division back to Origen, from whom then both the orders of the senses of Scripture can be seen to have derived.

A twofold distinction between the literal and the allegorical, the latter comprising what we usually call the allegorical, then based on that the moral, and beyond that the anagogical. A twofold distinction between the literal and the allegorical, the letter and the spirit, shadow and reality, the old and the new: this is, in fact, de Lubac insists, the distinction between the two testaments, the old and the new—this is the fundamental contrast that lies behind the distinction between the literal and the allegorical. Distinction, or perhaps better: movement, for it is the movement from old to new, a movement of fulfilment, not of change simply, or progress. Rather it is a movement to the new not simply as *novum*, but as *novum et aeternum*, as *novissimum*, the last; it is this movement that is accomplished in the transition from the literal to the allegorical. A movement of fulfilment: and it is in Christ that we find this fulfilment, it is Christ who fulfils the old, it is Christ in whom the hints and guesses of the old are realized in the reality of the new and eternal. The movement from the literal sense to the allegorical is a movement of understanding the mystery which the facts revealed by the literal sense disclose. 'Factum audivimus: mysterium requiramus' (we have heard the fact, let us seek the mystery—*In Jn.* 50.6), proclaims St. Augustine: the mystery which is the mystery of Christ. Understood like this, the movement to allegory is not at all a movement *away from* history, but we might say a movement into history, into the significance of the sacred events that are the object of our faith. The literal sense is the object of faith: this is what we are to believe, to believe *in,* in a God who meets us in history, becomes man in Jesus of Nazareth. The allegorical sense represents our attempt to understand the mystery we discern here. It is a movement from *fides* to *intelligentia*: de Lubac

---

[32] *Exégèse Médiévale*, I/1, p. 203.

remarks that the context of the Augustinian 'fides quaerens intellectum' is mainly that of the interpretation of the Scriptures.

The sort of insistence that I am putting now on the genuine significance of the historical is sometimes expressed in terms not of allegory, but of *typology*. Any who heard the late Cardinal Jean Daniélou speak on the subject will not easily forget that for him there was a very sharp distinction to be drawn between allegory and typology, and allegory was a bad thing, typology a good thing. He held the heart of the difference to be that allegory is concerned with *words*, typology with *events*; allegory elides history, typology is rooted in history. There is doubtless something of a distinction here, but I would not want to follow Daniélou and express the difference by the words 'allegory' and 'typology'. For two reasons: first, because in defending allegory I am seeking to defend an aspect of the thought of the Fathers and early medieval theologians, and though I would argue that they do anticipate the distinction Daniélou and others indicate by the words 'allegory' and 'typology' (that is, I hope, implicit in the way I presented their use of allegory, for in their hands it is not simply a literary device), they do not express it by these words. What Daniélou calls 'typology' they call 'allegory' (this is particularly true of the Latin tradition), and we are all set to misunderstand them if we restrict the reference of the term 'allegory' to something opposed to typology. ('Typology' is in fact a very recent coinage: the use of the Latin word *typologia* dates from around 1840, and the English 'typology' from 1844, according to Charity.[33])

But there is another reason for not following Daniélou in this usage, for the distinction is anyway not as sharp as he would make it: it is not a distinction between bare events and simple words at all. The 'types' of the Old Testament are not simply events, but the stories of the events and the significance that is attributed to them in their narration. The Exodus, for example, is a 'type' as a decisive event in the formation of the people of Israel. If the events that lie behind the Old Testament account were to turn out to be a rather unimportant episode in the remote history of some primitive Semitic tribe that later found its identity within the people of Israel, then such a bare un-

[33] A. C. Charity, *Events and their Afterlife* (Cambridge, 1966), p. 171 n.

varnished event could not form the type fulfilled in the New Testament: it is the event with the significance that it has received in the life of the People of Israel, as seen in the psalms and the prophets, and ultimately in the narrative that forms part of the book of Exodus.

The distinction indicated by the opposition of allegory and typology is, it seems to me, better characterized by the distinction Henri de Lubac draws between *allegoria facti* and *allegoria verbi*.[34] This is clearly a distinction between different types or styles of allegory, and it is *allegoria facti* that is fundamental. *Allegoria verbi* is only justified as a kind of embroidery of allegory of fact, not as a freely created, merely literary, conceit. De Lubac's standing example of *allegoria verbi*, as pure literary conceit, an example he abhors, is the allegory of the 'two swords', based on Luke 22:38, which was interpreted as justifying the doctrine of the 'two swords', that is, of ecclesiastical power wielded by the Pope and of temporal power wielded by the sovereign. For de Lubac this word-play has no basis in any *allegoria facti*: it is in no way an attempt to penetrate more deeply into the mystery of Christ. An example of how the two types of allegory relate to and mutually support one another can be seen in the traditional interpretation (going back to St. Paul and given significant development by St. Irenaeus) of Christ as the Second Adam. Christ reverses the work of Adam; Redemption remedies the Fall. Mary's obedience answers to Eve's disobedience; the tree, the wood, that provided the apple which occasioned the Fall has its work undone in the wood of the cross, the tree on which the world's Redeemer hung:

> ipse lignum tunc notavit,
> damna ligni ut solveret.

> (he then chose a tree,
> to undo the harm wrought by a tree.)

So far *allegoria facti* and *allegoria verbi* mutually inform one another. The way some of the Fathers draw together many different Scriptural references to 'wood' and build up an elaborate mosaic is more purely *allegoria verbi*, but it only

---

[34] See *Exégèse Médiévale*, II/2, pp. 131-40.

becomes arbitrary if it loses all contact with the fundamental *allegoria facti*, the fact in this case being the cross of Christ.

This movement from faith to understanding is not simply an intellectual process; it is not simply a matter of the development of doctrine. It is a matter of realizing our participation in the mystery of Christ. This has a dogmatic dimension, certainly, and this is the first to be developed: by the *allegoria* of the traditional way of interpreting Scripture. But these dogmas are not lifeless propositions: they disclose to us the lineaments of the mystery of Christ; and that mystery draws us to itself, that mystery invites our response. The allegorical sense leads into the moral sense. 'Historia et parabolis nutrimur; allegoria crescimus; moralitate perficimur' (by history and parables we are nourished; by allegory we grow; by morality we are perfected).[35] The Old Testament builds up a context, a matrix, in which the mystery of Christ can be incarnated. To become man is not just a physical fact, but a cultural event: in the Old Testament the cultural matrix is developed in which this can be possible. In the New Testament there is fulfilment: the mystery becomes a fact. And this mystery become fact transforms the whole of history: 'the summit of history, the fact of Christ presupposed history, and its radiance transfigured history,' says de Lubac,[36] and Hort echoes him: 'Out of Christ all that is behind is dead. We cannot legitimately knit together moment to moment or limb to limb. But in Him the whole dead past becomes alive again: it is part of His body and His life flows through every part.'[37]

It is this *newness* that allegory grasps as it seeks to interpret the Scriptures. But that mystery has to be fulfilled in us; we have to enter into that history. What was done in Christ is not past, but present in the One who is risen. 'The outward face of the mystery has passed, like everything that belongs to time—Christ entered into his glory and no longer suffers, no longer dies—but the inward face remains: as St. Leo put it, *Pascha Domini non tantum praeteritum recoli quam praesens debet honorari* (the Lord's passover is not so much recalled as past as honoured as present).'[38] And in this eternally present, not timeless, mystery we are called to participate. 'If it is true', says de Lubac, 'that

---

[35] Hugh of Rouen, quoted by de Lubac, I/2, p. 556.
[36] Ibid., I/2, p. 520.;
[37] *The Way, The Truth, The Life*, p. 181.
[38] *Exégèse Médiévale*, II/2, p. 122.

nothing is superior to the mystery of Christ, one must not forget that this mystery, which was prefigured in the Old Testament, is still realized, actualized, and achieved in the Christian soul. *Vere impletur in nobis.*'[39]

Understood like this it can hardly be claimed that allegory is arbitrary: allegory is firmly related to the mystery of Christ, it is a way of relating the whole of Scripture to that mystery, a way of making a synthetic vision out of the images and events of the Biblical narrative. It does not *prove* anything, but it is not meant to. The Fathers always bring forward allegorical interpretations tentatively, they recognize that other ways of interpretation, other applications of the allegorical approach, are possible, that there are different ways in which Scripture can be rightly taken. The literal meaning is the fundamental meaning: it is this that we are seeking to understand. Indeed the literal meaning of the *New* Testament is itself spiritual, it is the record of the fulfilment: it is *novissimum,* not just *novum.* The Fathers only allegorize, broadly speaking, in the case of the New Testament writings when it is a matter of stories and names that they regard as intended symbolically. Parables, obviously, and also names like Bethesda and Bethlehem and Peter—and, of course, numbers. The core of revealed fact is certainly to be understood more deeply and entered into, but it is not regarded as figurative. But to understand the Old Testament in the light of Christ —to understand it as the *Old* Testament—is to understand it figuratively, and allegory helps us to arrange these types and figures. As Paul Claudel put it, 'thus around the imperative and literal sense we learn that there exists a *field* of figures (one could say: *a magnetic field*), that is to say of resemblances and analogies oriented in a manner more or less direct and organic towards revealed and confirmed fact.'[40] The idea of a *magnetic field* is an attractive one: one could develop the analogy by thinking of the mystery of Christ as the magnetic pole and the field of force as the *regula fidei,* the rule of faith, in the context of which the Scriptures are to be interpreted and which is itself derived from the Scriptures. Keble puts it thus in his tract:

The Catholic Faith, the Mind of Christ testified by His universal Church, limits the range of symbolical interpretation ... in Scripture

---

[39] Ibid. I/2, p. 557.   [40] Op. cit. (n. 5), p. 20.

... as St Augustin again expresses it, 'We that are made the Body of Christ, let us not fail to recognize our own voice in the Psalms and other Scriptures: our own voice, because it is the Voice of Him in whom we are all made one. 'Christ', he proceeds, 'wheresoever in those Books, wheresoever in the Scriptures I am journeying and panting for breath, in that sweat of our face which is part of our sentence as men—Christ is there, openly or secretly to meet and re- fresh me. It is He Himself, who, by the very difficulty which I some- times have in finding Him, inflames my longing, so that what I do find of His I may eagerly suck in, and retain to my soul's health, absorbed in the very joints and marrow.' ... In other words, the analogy of faith, Christ set before us in the Creed of the Church, will give a fixedness and reality to our symbolical interpretations, how wide soever in other respects the latitude and variety which seems to be allowed in them.[41]

Claudel too writes of hearing in Scripture the voice of a Father who speaks to us, and states that in hearing this voice which made me I recognize not just the voice of the spirit, but what the simple rightly call 'la voix du sang.'[42]

It is in the liturgy *par excellence* that the allegorical way comes into its own. For in the liturgy the mystery of Christ, the paschal mystery, is celebrated and adored, and the readings from Scrip- ture, combined with the liturgical year which concentrates successively on different aspects of the mystery always cele- brated, draw out of the mystery the wealth and variety of its signification. The prophets, the wandering of the children of Israel in the wilderness, the life of the early Church, the sacred events of the Incarnation themselves, are seen in relation to the mystery celebrated in our midst and invite and interpret our participation. And in this we see that the way of allegory is a way of prayer, the prayer of the Church and the prayer of each one of us with the Church, *anima ecclesiastica*.

It may be useful here to give an extended example of the way 'allegory' can open up the theological significance of a biblical passage. The example I choose is the account of the baptism of Jesus, when, according to the accounts in the Gospels, as he rose out of the water, the heavens were opened, the Spirit descended on Jesus in the form of a dove, and there was a voice from heaven

[41] Keble (n. 3), p. 182.
[42] Claudel (n. 5), p. 21.

saying, 'This is my beloved Son' (Matt. 3:16-17; or Mark 1: 10-11; Luke 3:21-2). The Fathers regularly intepret this as a revelation of the Trinity, seeing in the voice from heaven the Father, the Spirit in the dove descending, and the Son in the man, Jesus. So, for instance, Origen in his commentary on Luke says:

Because therefore the Lord has been baptized and the heavens have been opened and the Holy Spirit descended on him and a voice from heaven sounded, saying, 'This is my beloved Son, in whom I am well pleased', it is to be said that by the baptism of Jesus the heaven has been pierced and that,the heaven thus opened, the Holy Spirit has descended for the dispensation of the remission of sins, not of him who did no sin neither was any guile found in his mouth, but of all the world, that, after the Lord has ascended up on high leading captivity captive, he might give us the Spirit ... The Holy Spirit however descended on the Saviour in the form of a dove, a gentle bird, innocent and simple. Whence we are commanded to imitate the innocency of the dove. Such too is the Holy Spirit, pure and winged, ascending on high. Why in prayer do we say: who will give me wings like a dove that I might fly away and be at peace?, that is: who will give me the wings of the Holy Spirit? And in another place the prophetic word is pleased to say: if you have rested in the inheritance, you will have the silvered wings of a dove, with its back in the splendour of gold. For if we have rested among the inheritance of the Old and the New Testaments, there will be given to us the silvered wings of a dove, that is the words of God, his back radiant with shining gold and splendour so that our sense may be infused with the senses of the Holy Spirit, that is, that word and mind may be fulfilled by his coming and we may not speak something we do not understand, except at his suggestion, and all sanctification in Christ Jesus may come, as to our heart, so too to our words and deeds by the Holy Spirit ...[43]

Here Origen sees in the baptism of our Lord part of the decisive significance of the Incarnation: the heavens are now open to man, the Holy Spirit descends and man is accepted with God, that is, forgiven. Origen develops the significance of the coming of the Holy Spirit by exploring some of the symbolic meaning of the dove, and does this by referring back to the Scriptural understanding of the dove as innocent and gentle (itself a commonplace of ancient natural history), and as a bird that soars lightly into the skies: and as the allegory opens up the significance of this

[43] *Hom.* XXVII; *GCS* pp. 159-60.

passage, we see how we are to respond to it—with a response of innocence and a soaring desire for God.

Much the same picture can be found elsewhere in the Fathers. For instance, we find Chrysostom saying: 'For what reason did the Holy Spirit appear in the form of a dove? Because the living and pure one is gentle. Since the Holy Spirit is the spirit of gentleness, because of this he appeared thus. But further, because, after the flood, the dove proclaimed the release from the storm, bearing a branch of olive. For the Holy Spirit now brings the release from evil and, instead of the branch of the olive, brings a sign of freedom for all ...'.[44] The reference back to the dove which Noah released from the ark, and which announced the end of the flood by bringing an olive-branch, adds a further symbolic colour to the significance of the baptism of our Lord. Cyril of Alexandria, in the fragment of his commentary on Luke preserved in the *catena* on that Gospel, says of our Lord at his baptism: 'He opened the heavens, which the first Adam had shut up, showing how the power of baptism effects an ascent to heaven ... If it is said that the Spirit descended as a dove, this shows clearly the unity of the Old and New Covenants of God; and this by a reminder of the flood that took place under Noah. For as then a dove announced the ceasing of God's wrath, so now the form of a dove announces the fall due to sin and the redemption of the world ...'.[45]

Augustine, in his sermon on Matthew's account of the Baptism, sees here a clear manifestation of the doctrine of the Trinity: 'we have therefore in a certain way the Trinity in its distinctions: in the voice, the Father; in the man, the Son; in the dove, the Spirit.'[46] However, as the rest of the sermon goes on to explain, an explanation Augustine returns to in his *De Trinitate*, the Son is in the man in a uniquely real manner, whereas the voice and the dove merely symbolize the Father and the Spirit. It is a point Chrysostom too notes: 'if the Holy Spirit appeared in the vision of a dove, it is necessary to know that he did not take the nature of a dove, as the Son of God took the nature of a man: whence also the Evangelist does not say "in the nature of a

---

[44] Quoted from the Greek *catena* on Matthew, in J. A. Cramer, *Catenae Graecorum Patrum in Novum Testamentum* (Oxford, 1844), vol. I, p. 24.

[45] Ibid. II.32.

[46] Sermon LII; *PL* 38.355.

dove'' but ''in the form of a dove''.'[47] In his *De Trinitate* Augustine puts the point thus: 'a creature, in which the Holy Spirit appears, is not so assumed as was that flesh and human form that was taken from the Virgin Mary. For the Spirit did not make blessed that dove, or that wind, or that fire, and he did not join himself and his person to it in a unity and possession forever';[48] or a little later: 'the form of the servant inhered in the unity of person, but these corporeal forms had appeared to show what was the work at that time, and afterwards ceased.'[49]

This, perhaps, enables us to bring into sharper focus de Lubac's point, referred to earlier, that the spiritual meaning of the New Testament *is* the literal meaning. In what Jesus was and did—at his baptism, in this instance, and even more in what that foreshadowed—we have not a symbol of something else, but that to which all the symbols refer. And the symbols are present in this passage—in the voice and the dove—as providing the frame, as it were, in which we can see the significance of the events: they 'show what was the work at the time and afterwards ceased'. The spiritual meaning of the New Testament is the history of the Incarnate One, a history which is 'a new and living way, which he hath consecrated for us, through the veil, that is to say, his flesh' (Heb. 10:20)—a way which we are all to enter upon and tread.

And it is, of course, our baptism and the life of faith, hope, and love to which it commits us that provide our entrance into the history of Jesus. So the themes that have just been outlined are naturally picked up in the baptismal liturgies of the Church, and in the Church's celebration of the feast of the Baptism of our Lord. So, for instance, in this prayer from the *Liber Ordinum* for the blessing of the font, the voice and the descent of the Spirit are picked up, as also is the theme of the opening of heaven and the restoration of Paradise: 'May the voice of thy divinity sound upon these waters, may the Spirit of thy sanctification dwell therein and bring healing to all ills. May the abundant streams of paradise flow from it, that by thy goodness heavenly graces may be bestowed upon these new-born children ...'.[50] So, too, in the

[47] Cramer (n. 44), I.24-5.
[48] *De Trinitate*, II.vi.11.
[49] Ibid., II.vii.12.
[50] E. C. Whitaker, *Documents of the Baptismal Liturgy* (London, 1960), p. 115.

dismissal hymn for the feast of the Epiphany in the Byzantine Rite (in which the Baptism of our Lord is as much the subject of the celebration as his Manifestation): 'When Thou, O Lord, wast baptized in Jordan, the worship of the Trinity was made manifest. The voice of the Father bore witness to Thee, and called Thee His Beloved Son; and the Spirit, in the form of a dove, confirmed the immutability of the words. O Christ our God, who didst appear and illuminate the world: glory to Thee.'[51]

In the Baptism of our Lord, then, the Trinity is made manifest. And it is worth noting that it is made manifest in the declaration of the *Son*: it is the Sonship of Jesus that reveals to us the mystery of the Trinity. And as he is revealed to us as the Son, so we are reminded of our calling to be 'sons in the Son' by the grace of the Holy Spirit. So it is in the Fathers' interpretation of this passage that the emphasis falls on sonship, displayed in the form of the servant, a sonship in which we are to participate, and on the descent of the Spirit as a dove, for it is through the Spirit that we become sons and are enabled to call upon God as Father.

There is a final example of this tradition that can be cited: from the writings of Jeremy Taylor, the Caroline divine who lived from 1613 to 1667, ending his life as Bishop of Down and Connor, and of Dromore. Jeremy Taylor is particularly interesting in this context, for his *Life of Christ* is a sustained example of the kind of exegesis that has been discussed in this chapter. Each section of the work is divided into three: first a retelling of the history of the episode involved, so it is made clear that the literal sense is the foundation of the work; then a meditation, which opens up the allegorical significance of the passage and sees within that the nature of our response—so in the meditation we pass from the allegorical to the moral sense, in the way de Lubac holds before us as traditional; all this is then summed up in the final section which takes the form of a prayer. And there is another point to be made: we have seen how the allegorical sense comes into its own in the liturgy. With the Caroline divines we find that what would have happened in the liturgy passes over into the sermon—or the kind of extension of a sermon that such a

---

[51] *The Divine Liturgy of St. John Chrysostom* (Faith Press, London, no date), p.129.

work as the *Life of Christ* represents. It is easy to see why. The liturgy of the Church of England had been greatly simplified at the Reformation: gone were the hymns and antiphons that had picked up the allegorical significance of the texts used in the celebration of the feasts of the Church. The basic materials were still there, the Scriptures and the Psalter, and were indeed prayed and read more thoroughly than ever before; the cycle of the Church's year was preserved, and indeed emerged in greater clarity, and it was in this context that the Scriptures were read and the psalms recited; the collects and other prayers still provided a crucible in which the considerations of the several feasts were fused into prayer. But it was the sermon now that provided the opportunity for the allegorical theological significance of the Scriptural passages to be brought out: and the Caroline divines responded with enthusiasm to the opportunity. It is this, it seems to me, that lies behind the richness and breadth of Taylor's style, providing, as it were, a space in which the allegorical significance could develop and expand, and men's minds and hearts be drawn into the mystery of Christ thus displayed.

So Jeremy Taylor introduces his theme, when he comments on Jesus' meeting with John the Baptist and John's baptizing of Jesus:

And this was the greatest meeting that ever was upon earth, where the whole cabinet of the mysterious Trinity was opened and shewn, as much as the capacities of our present imperfections will permit; the second person in veil of humanity, the third in the shape or with the motion of a dove; but the first kept His primitive state; and as to the Israelites He gave nótice by way of caution. 'Ye saw no shape, but ye heard a voice,' so now also God the Father gave testimony to His holy Son and appeared, only in a voice without any visible representment.[52]

It is interesting to recall here that from 1549 until the revised lectionary of 1871 the third chapter of St. Matthew's Gospel, including the account of our Lord's Baptism, was ordered to be read at Mattins on Trinity Sunday (in 1871 it became, for some reason, on optional reading at Evensong): so there is added

---

[52] *The Whole Works of the Rt Revd Jeremy Taylor,* ed. R. Heber, rev. C. P. Eden (London, 1847), vol. II, p. 191. Cf. with this the use of the imagery of the 'cabinet' in George Herbert's poem 'Ungratefulness'.

significance in the way Taylor thus first brings out the Trinitarian dimension of the Baptism. Taylor goes on to draw out the meaning of Christ's Baptism by seeing it, as the Fathers did, as the baptism of the One into whom we are baptized:

After the holy Jesus was baptized, and had prayed, the heavens opened, the holy Ghost descended, and a voice from heaven proclaimed Him to be the Son of God, and one in whom the Father was well pleased; and the same ointment that was cast upon the head of our High priest, went unto His beard, and thence fell to the borders of His garment: for as Christ our Head felt these effects in manifestation, so the church believes God does to her and to her meanest children, in the susception of the holy rite of baptism in right, apt, and holy dispositions. For the heavens open too upon us; and the holy Ghost descends, to sanctify the waters, and to hallow the catechumen, and to pardon the past and repented sins, and to consign him to the inheritance of sons, and to put on his military girdle, and give him the sacrament and oath of fidelity ...[53]

He comments too on the descent of the Spirit in the form of a dove 'whose proprieties of nature are pretty and modest hieroglyphics of the duty of spiritual persons':

The dove sings not, but mourns; it hath no gall, strikes not with its bill, hath no crooked talons, and forgets its young ones soonest of any of the inhabitants of the air. And the effects of the holy Spirit are symbolical in all the sons of sanctification: for the voice of the church is sad in those accents which express her own condition; but as the dove is not so sad in her breast as in her note, so neither is the interior condition of the church wretched and miserable, but indeed her song is most of it elegy within her own walls; and her condition looks sad, and her joys are not pleasures in the public estimate, but they that afflict her think her miserable because they know not the sweetness of a holy peace and serenity which supports her spirit, and plains the heart under a rugged brow, making the soul festival under the noise of a threne and sadder groanings ... But besides this hieroglyphical representment, this dove, like that which Noah sent out from the ark, did aptly signify the world to be renewed, and all to be turned to a new creation; and God hath made a new covenant with us, that unless we provoke Him He will never destroy us any more.[54]

Here, then, we see the last echoes of the tradition we have found in the Fathers—a tradition that was soon to die out, at

---

[53] Ibid., p. 196.   [54] Ibid., pp. 196-7.

least for a time: for the sermon was to cease to feel the pressure of
the Church's experience of Scripture—an experience well
characterized by H. E. Allen when she says of Richard Rolle
(one of the first in England to make known the riches of the
Church's experience of Scripture to those who were limited to
the vernacular): 'To Rolle [the Scriptures] had been sacred
drama, on which to feed his spiritual life.'[55] And as the sermon
ceased to feel this pressure, it degenerated into a moral discourse.[56]

But the tradition cannot be completely lost, and it is interesting to note the way in which more modern methods of interpreting Scripture, with their close attention to the use of
individual words, have opened up new insights into the mystery
of the presence of the Old Testament in the New. A good
example can be found in interpretations of the narrative of our
Lady's Visitation of Elizabeth. When Elizabeth hears Mary's
greeting, the baby John the Baptist, still in her womb, leaps for
joy. Max Thurian comments: 'John the Baptist is like David
who danced and leapt with joy before the Ark of the Covenant at
the entering-in of Jerusalem (2 Sam. 6:16; 1 Chron. 15:29).
The Son of God in Mary produces in her a kind of messianic
exaltation, even as the sacred Presence in the Ark calls King
David to dance and tumble with joy.'[57] It is indeed a commonplace nowadays to note that the word for joy here (*agalliasis*) is
an unusual word which in the Septuagint has the special
meaning of exultation at the approach of the Messiah and the
Messianic age.[58] Neither of these points—the comparison of
John the Baptist with David, and the realization that John's
joy is messianic—is found, so far as I am aware, in those we are
accustomed to call the 'Fathers', yet they seem to me to be
fundamentally in the tradition of the Fathers, and indeed a
genuine enrichment of that tradition.[59]

[55] Introduction to *English Writings of Richard Rolle*, ed. H. E. Allen (Oxford, 1931),
p. lviii.
[56] See Charles Smyth, *The Art of Preaching* (London, 1940), especially chapter VI:
'The Triumph of Tillotson'.
[57] *Mary: Mother of the Lord, Figure of the Church* (London, 1963), p. 67.
[58] See W. F. Arndt and F. W. Gingrich, *A Greek-English Lexicon of the New Testament*
(Chicago and Cambridge, 1957), s.v.
[59] Cf. G. Florovsky's discussion of the notion of the 'Fathers' in the theology and his
insistence that the 'Age of the Fathers' cannot be restricted to some past historical
epoch: in *Bible, Church, Tradition: An Eastern Orthodox View* (vol. 1 of his Collected Works,
Belmont, Mass., 1972), pp. 100-12.

In Augustine's exposition of the principles of exegesis in his
On Christian Doctrine, an exposition rare among the Fathers, we
find what might seem at first sight a strange contrast. On the one
hand, there is a good deal of complexity about the methods used
in interpreting the Scriptures. A good deal of learning is
required (and though it looks superficial to us, in his own day it
was probably fairly elaborate), the ways of interpreting the
words of Scripture and the use of allegory are explained at some
length. On the other hand, we are told repeatedly that Scripture
teaches nothing but charity: 'the plenitude and the end ... of all
the sacred Scriptures is the love of a Being which is to be enjoyed
and of a being which can share that enjoyment with us ...'[60]. The
message of the Scriptures is of the utmost simplicity: love. It is
not difficult to understand this contrast; Augustine would
probably feel that the Scriptures themselves make it abundantly
clear. For they begin with an account of man's creation and fall,
and in man's fall all becomes complicated. Man falls from
simplicity to confusion and multiplicity—into the 'land of
unlikeness' (*regio dissimilitudinis*) as Augustine puts it.[61] The
simple, clear crystal of love is shattered into countless pieces: we
can no longer see how they fit together.[62] The Scriptures tell the
story of God's way of leading men back into unity, and the way
has to be from the fragmented to the unified. The history of the
Old Testament fashions a matrix, a kaleidoscope, which shares
in our fragmentedness and yet harks forward to the simplicity of
the One who will restore all things, the One 'in quo omnia
constant'. And we need not doubt that it is the *history* of the Old
Testament that does this, for as St. Thomas Aquinas put it,
'auctor rerum non solum potest verba accommodare ad aliquid
significandum: sed etiam res potest disponere in figuram
alterius' (the author of all things can not only arrange words to
signify something, but also dispose things to be the figure of
something else).[63]

And it is allegory that enables us to discern this pattern, and
not only discern it but by means of this pattern restore within

---

[60] *On Christian Doctrine,* I.xxxv.39 (Robertson, p. 30).
[61] *Confessions,* VII.x.16.
[62] Cf. Peter Brown's remarks on Augustine's use of allegory, in *Augustine of Hippo* (London, 1967), pp. 261-2.
[63] *Quodlibet.* IX.7.a.14: quoted by Claudel (n. 5), p. 90.

ourselves the unity and simplicity lost by the Fall, and so come again to love. The heart of Scripture is the end of Scripture: the love of God in Christ calling us to respond to that love. Pascal summed up well the core of the way of allegory in these words from his *Pensées*:

> Tout ce qui ne va point à la charité est figuré.
> L'unique objet de l'Écriture est la charité.
>
> (Everything that does not lead to love is figurative.
> The sole object of Scripture is love.)[64]

---

[64] *Pensées* 270 (Lafuma edn. no. 670 in Brunschvicg).

VI. LIVING THE MYSTERY

WE began by dwelling on the phenomenon of division, failure to relate, 'dissociation of sensibility', that seems to characterize much of our contemporary awareness, and from that point on we have tried to understand how this division is perpetuated and driven deeper in our search for knowledge and understanding. In doing this we have tried to catch some glimpse, some understanding, of the lost unity and to see some way of attaining it again. It the first three chapters we explored a division between science and the humanities and the way in which the very success of the sciences has tended to seduce the humanities into aping sciences—a process which, far from healing any division, has only made it worse. Following Gadamer and others, we have seen in the sciences and their success the manifestation of the self-confidence of the Enlightenment's search for objective truth through the employment of a method, and I have suggested that far from the humanities needing to develop any similar techniques, they have their own approach to knowledge which is betrayed if they seek to ape the sciences. I have argued too that theology is, not surprisingly, a part of the older way of attaining knowledge and that it betrays itself if it seeks to become 'scientific' by any attempt to fashion an objective scientific method. In all this I had in mind, at least partly, the seductive claims of the so-called historical-critical method, and its use in theology (and other disciplines) over the last century and a half. We then briefly looked at criticism of the 'scientific method' itself by scientists, especially Michael Polanyi, and noted that, if correct, it would follow that there is a much closer analogy between ways of knowing in the sciences and the humanities, but that in this case it is not the sciences that provide the paradigm, but rather the humanities themselves. This encouraged us to think that some attempt to dig more deeply into the traditional structure of theology, as found in the Fathers, might provide some insight into the nature of the unity we have lost and which we seek. There followed chapters discussing tradition, not simply as an element in theology—a

kind of source material—but as opening up the whole enterprise
of theology and disclosing its proper concerns; and on allegory,
as a method of interpreting Scripture. Here, besides looking at
something that is almost universally ignored in current theological effort, we found that sympathetic understanding of it
disclosed dimensions of the theological task often ignored,
which, if taken into account, could restore to the theological
task greater coherence and unity. We noted in particular the way
in which allegory draws back into the centre of the concerns of
theology the liturgy and the spiritual life and so discloses a
unity between theology and prayer and worship not always very
evident in the theology of more recent times.

It has been an attempt to understand division and an effort to
achieve—or at least discern—a unity transcending such division. To take our discussion further and to draw it to a close, we
might now look at an earlier attempt to reach behind division
and find a deeper unity. We refer to Baron von Hügel's great
work *The Mystical Element of Religion*,[1] which explored many
kinds of division and their resolution in the life of the Church
and the life of the saint. But he began by drawing attention to one
manifestation of division in particular:

Amongst the apparent enigmas of life, amongst the seemingly most
radical and abiding of interior antinomies and conflicts experienced by
the human race and by individuals, there is one which everything tends
to make us feel and see with an ever-increasing keenness and clearness.
More and more we want a strong and interior, a lasting yet voluntary
bond of union between our own successive states of mind, and between
what is abiding in ourselves and what is permanent within our fellow-
men; and more and more we seem to see that mere Reasoning, Logic,
Abstraction,—all that appears as the necessary instrument and
expression of the Universal and Abiding—does not move or win the
will, either in ourselves or in others; and that what does thus move and
win it, is Instinct, Intuition, Feeling, the Concrete and Contingent, all
that seems to be of its very nature individual and evanescent. Reasoning appears but capable, at best, of co-ordinating, unifying, explaining
the material furnished to it by experience of all kinds; at worst, of explaining it away; at best, of stimulating the purveyance of a fresh supply
of such experience; at worst, of stopping such purveyance as much as
may be. And yet the Reasoning would appear to be the transferable

[1] Second edn., London, 1923.

part in the process, but not to move us; and the experience alone to
have the moving power, but not to be transmissible.[2]

And a little later on he refers to this 'apparent interior antinomy'
as being between 'the particular concrete experience which
alone moves us and helps to determine our will, but which,
seemingly, is untransferable, indeed unrepeatable; and the
general, abstract reasoning which *is* repeatable, indeed transferable, but which does not move us or help directly to determine
the will.'[3] This, along with many other problems all bound up
with it and informing it, is the subject of von Hügel's reflections in the two dense volumes of his *Mystical Element*. At the end
of volume 1, he feels able to offer the 'general outlines of the
true answer to this pressing question'. He begins by saying:

Only a life sufficiently large and alive to take up and retain, within its
own experimental range, at least some of the poignant question and
conflict, as well as of the peace-bringing solution and calm: hence a
life dramatic with a humble and homely heroism which, in rightful
contact with and in rightful renunciation of the Particular and Fleeting, ever seeks and finds the Omnipresent and Eternal; and which
again deepens and incarnates (for its own experience and apprehension and for the stimulation of other souls) this Transcendence in
its own thus gradually purified Particular: only such a life can be
largely persuasive, at least for us Westerns and in our times.[4]

The solution is not some theoretical resolution but—put
briefly—the life of a saint, and von Hügel has gained this
insight through his attempt (which is the ostensible subject of the
book) to understand the life of the late fifteenth-century Italian
mystic, Catherine of Genoa. We can see something more of his
meaning if we recall one of the things he says about religion in
the introductory pages of volume 1:

For religion is ever, *qua* religion, authoritative and absolute. What
constitutes religion is not simply to hold a view and to try to live a
life, with respect to the Unseen and the Deity, as possibly or even
certainly beautiful or true or good: but precisely that which is over and
above this,—the holding this view and this life to proceed somehow
from God Himself, so as to bind my innermost mind and conscience to

[2] Ibid., vol. I, p. 3.
[3] Ibid., I, p. 10.
[4] Ibid., I, p. 368.

unhesitating assent. Not simply that I think it, but that, in addition, I feel bound to think it, transforms thought about God into a religious act.[5]

And the saint is one in whom this religious act has become steady and fundamental: and it too is something learnt, something made one's own, not simply something entertained on the surface of one's mind. As von Hügel says, 'the further the soul advances, the more it sees and realizes the profound truth, that all it does and is, is somehow given to it; and hence that, inasmuch as it is permanent at all, it is grounded upon, environed, supported, penetrated and nourished by Him who is its origin and its end. Here all the soul's actions tend to coalesce to simply being, and this being, in so far as there and then acceptable to the conscience, comes more and more to be felt and considered as the simple effect of the one direct action of God alone.'[6] This is not something attained all at once; it is not even something seen all at once and then made one's own. Rather, as von Hügel says, 'without much dim apprehension, no clear perception; nothing is more certain than this.'[7] The soul must pass through the stage of 'dim apprehension', where it must trust and endure; there is no quick and direct route to 'clear apprehension'. This recalls the distinction between first and second clearness that von Hügel made in one of his letters to his niece— two clarities, of which only the final one is of any enduring value: 'nothing in philosophy, still more in religion, should ever be attempted in and with the first clearness ..., but in and with the *second clearness*, which only comes after that first cheery clarity has gone, and has been succeeded by a dreary confusion and obtuseness of mind. Only this second clearness, rising up, like something in no wise one's own, from the depths of one's subconsciousness—only this is any good in such great matters ...'.[8] That is a familiar experience, but it is less common to see its fundamental significance and to hold to it as a basic truth—as does von Hügel.

A division between the rational, communicable but superficial,

---

[5] Ibid. I, p. 46.
[6] Ibid., I, p. 369.
[7] Ibid. II, p. 265.
[8] Gwendolen Greene (ed.), *Letters from Baron von Hügel to a Niece* (London, 1928), p. 74.

and the intuitive, which moves us and determines our will, but which is incommunicable—a division between the objective and the subjective as Kierkegaard understood that distinction—resolved at the level of the saint, or more exactly at the level of the saintly *life*, resolved not in a concept, but in a life, or an act, or a succession of acts, acts which are lived not in a clarity they attain to, but through a darkness and confusion of 'dim apprehension'. It seems to me that this draws together some of the themes we have been considering and points us to a more fundamental unity. Maybe, too, it administers a corrective to some of the one-sidedness we may seem to have yielded to in our exploration. For instance, the attentive reader may have sensed something of a wrong note at the beginning of chapter III when I argued against the affinity of theology with the sciences by saying that theologians work in libraries, not in laboratories; they read books, they do not conduct experiments: for this conveys a too exclusively academic and intellectual understanding of theology; it forgets the ideal of some of the (usually much despised) Protestant scholastics of theology as 'sapientia eminens practica,'[9] a supremely *practical* wisdom; it is too distanced from Evagrius' ideal of the theologian as 'one who prays truly', an activity which, for Evagrius, is prepared for and tested by the life of the virtues, a life of asceticism. Though it is true that theologians work in libraries, rather than laboratories, and that libraries contain the monument to their achievement—something Newman expresses with well-judged irony when he says of the Christian faith: 'To see its triumph over the world's wisdom, we must enter those solemn cemeteries in which are stored the relics and monuments of the ancient faith—our libraries'[10]—we miss the true nature of theology if we do not see that many of these tomes contain sermons, conferences given to monks, letters written to those seeking spiritual guidance: in short, literature that was directly concerned with fostering the Christian life of those for whom it was intended. And this picks up quite immediately themes from the preceding chapters: the focusing of allegory in love, the expression of tradition in prayer,

[9] See, for instance, Carl Heinz Ratschow, *Lutherische Dogmatik zwischen Reformation und Aufklärung* (Gütersloh, 1964), Teil I, p. 42. The quotation in the text is from Hollaz.
[10] *Sermons, chiefly on the Theory of Religious Belief, preached before the University of Oxford* (London, 1843), p. 314.

and even my exposition of the thought of Gadamer. For Gadamer stresses the importance of *performance* in the matter of aesthetic judgement: in the case of a play, for example, to interpret it is, most crucially, to perform it: it is not a matter of attaining a simply conceptual understanding. So in the more general case of interpreting literary works, this involves not simply understanding and explaining, but also *application*; and as Gadamer develops this notion of application, we see that for him understanding a literary work is not a matter of gaining some conceptual understanding which the work enshrines and which is the same for everyone (something 'objective'), it is a matter of an experience that takes place in one's engagement with the work, an experience that brings understanding and insight into reality. It is, as Gadamer stresses, a process in which we are 'undeceived'—for 'every experience worthy of the name runs counter to our expectations'—undeceived of those of our prejudices that do not 'fit' reality.[11] And we have seen that Gadamer regards this process of undeception, which is the result of experience, as summed up in Aeschylus' *pathei mathos*, which, however, goes beyond undeception in any particular, for 'what a man has to learn through suffering is not this or that particular thing, but knowledge of the limitations of humanity, of the absoluteness of the barrier that separates him from the divine. It is ultimately a religious insight—the kind of insight which gave birth to Greek tragedy. Thus experience is experience of human finitude. The truly experienced man is one who is aware of this, who knows that he is master neither of time nor of the future ...'.[12]

This stress on performance, doing, act, is central to the understanding of the notion of faith Newman worked out in his *University Sermons,* and it will be worth exploring this somewhat here, as it brings into closer focus the ideas we have just looked at in Baron von Hügel, and brings out more clearly the way in which the discussion of this chapter recapitulates and crystallizes the concerns of this book. For Newman it is central to a true understanding of faith to see it as concerned with conduct, with action. It is not simply the entertaining of a view or an idea, but

---

[11] Gadamer, *Truth and Method*, p. 319.
[12] Ibid., p. 320.

the uniting of such a view or idea to the springs of one's action (a distinction Newman expressed in his *Grammar of Assent* as that between notional and real assent). So it is said, as Newman puts it, 'to be a venture, to involve a risk'.[13] From this central observation there flow various consequences, but to see how they flow we must first see that Newman does *not* mean, when he says that faith is concerned with conduct and must issue in conduct, that faith is not an intellectual act. Affirming that 'Reason is the faculty of the mind ... by which knowledge of things external to us, of beings, facts, and events, is attained beyond the range of sense,'[14] Newman argues that 'if this be Reason, an act or process of Faith, simply considered, is certainly an exercise of Reason ...'.[15] He argues elsewhere in the Sermons that 'even in the case of intellectual excellence, it is considered the highest of gifts to possess an intuitive knowledge of the beautiful in art, or the effective in action, without reasoning or investigating; that this, in fact, is *genius*; and that they who have a corresponding insight into moral truth (as far as they have it) have reached that especial perfection in the spiritual part of their nature, which is so rarely found, and so greatly prized among the intellectual endowments of the soul.'[16] What Newman is doing here is to explore the shallowness of the view that reduces the intellect to mere ratiocination, and to argue that the deepest level of the intellect transcends ratiocination and has an intuitive grasp of what it understands. He is seeking to show that it is what the Greeks called *nous* that is the deepest level of the intellect, and one wonders if Newman's insight here is not in some part the fruit of his deep knowledge of the Fathers (especially the Greek Fathers). But this deepest level of the intellect is not contemplative in any pejorative sense—simply content with beholding, inactive—rather it is essentially moral and issues in action. It is important to note here that Newman refused to accept the dichotomy between reason and will, which had been common in the West from the time of St. Bernard and which gained a new lease of life in the wake of Kant. Faith, which issues in conduct, is the concern of the intellectual faculty: it is indeed the most 'greatly prized among the intellectual endowments of

---

13 Newman (n. 10), p. 217.   14 Ibid., p. 198.
         15 Ibid., p. 199.   16 Ibid., p. 70.

the soul'. It is this dichotomy between reason and will that Newman regarded as the fundamental error of liberalism (something expressed with especial clarity in his essay on the *Tamworth Reading Room*) and in that he finds himself in the—at first sight unlikely—company of his contemporaries Marx and Kierkegaard.

But if faith is an intellectual act, it does not manifest its intellectuality (and rationality) in a concern for reasons and arguments and evidence. This is partly because the real reasons why we do things lie deep—'the multiform and intricate assemblage of considerations, which really lead to judgment and action, must be attenuated or mutilated' when they are reduced to 'a major and minor premiss'.[17] The reasoning that lies behind our actions is usually implicit, as Newman puts it, and can only rarely be made explicit. The desire to make all reasoning explicit manifests 'a dislike of an evidence, varied, minute, complicated, and a desire of something producible, striking, and decisive':[18] such a desire is really irrational, as it fails to understand the realities of human behaviour and action. 'To maintain that Faith is a judgement about facts in matters of conduct, such, as to be formed, not so much from the impression legitimately made upon the mind by those facts, as from the reaching out of the mind itself towards them,—that it is a presumption, not a proving—may sound paradoxical, yet surely is borne out by the actual state of things as they come before us every day ...'.[19]

In that reference to presumption rather than proving, Newman is pointing to the way in which faith differs from the ordinary exercise of reason in arguing from facts perceived to conclusions. Faith is less concerned with evidence than with anticipations and presumptions. It is not a passive reception of knowledge but an active 'reaching forward of the mind': 'mere evidence would but lead to passive opinions and knowledge: but anticipations and presumptions are the creation of the mind itself; and the faith which exists in them is of an active nature ...'.[20] Faith is, as it were, a skill and not a method like the 'scientific reason' with which Newman is contrasting it. This he brings out in the famous analogy of the climber in the thirteenth

[17] Ibid., p. 223.
[18] Ibid., p. 273.
[19] Ibid., pp. 217-18.
[20] Ibid., p. 219.

sermon, which actually describes Reason, in its fundamental
aspect—the aspect in which it is at one with faith, in contrast
with methodical, ratiocinative reason:

It makes progess not unlike a clamberer on a steep cliff, who, by quick
eye, prompt hand, and firm foot, ascends how he knows not himself,
by personal endowments and by practice, rather than by rule, leaving
no track behind him, and unable to teach another. It is not too much to
say that the stepping by which great geniuses scale the mountains of
truth is as unsafe and precarious to men in general, as the ascent of a
skilful mountaineer up a literal crag. It is a way which they alone can
take; and its justification lies in their success. And such mainly is the
way in which all men, gifted or not gifted, reason,—not by rule, but by
an inward faculty.[21]

And like a skill it is acquired by practice, and the practice here
is the practice of love, humility, trust in God: 'here a certain
moral state, and not evidence, is made the means of gaining the
Truth, and the beginning of spiritual perfection.'[22] So it is that
Newman insists that faith finds its safeguard not in reason, as a
bulwark against superstition, but in love, 'a right state of
heart'.[23] Newman sums up his understanding of faith thus:
'Right Faith is the faith of a right mind. Faith is an intellectual
act; right Faith is an intellectual act, done in a certain moral
disposition. Faith is an act of Reason, viz, a reasoning upon
presumptions; right Faith is a reasoning upon holy, devout, and
enlightened presumptions. Faith ventures and hazards; right
Faith ventures and hazards deliberately, seriously, soberly,
piously, and humbly, counting the cost and delighting in the
sacrifice.'[24]
    Newman's doctrine of faith can be seen, then, as a response to
the rationalism of the Enlightenment, and it is fascinating to
observe how surely it responds to those elements in the thought
of the Enlightenment which were highlighted in earlier chapters
as dissolving men's sense of tradition and solidarity with the
past. It is exactly the attempt to start from scratch, to build up a
faith for oneself from the evidences, that Newman has in his
sights; and it is precisely a sense of tradition, the idea of the
past as the bearer of those prejudices and presumptions that

[21] Ibid., pp. 252-3.   [22] Ibid., p. 231.
[23] Ibid., p. 230.   [24] Ibid., pp. 232-3.

enable us to attain understanding, that Newman defends. Against the idea of a method that anyone may, in principle, use to attain truth, Newman points to something less easy to define, something learnt by example, something rather like a skill or a developed insight or sensitivity working through sympathy, something whose archetype is not the clever arguing of a debater, but the humble understanding of the saint, whose faith is tested and proven in a life. So it is Mary, the Mother of God, who 'is our pattern of Faith, both in the reception and in the study of Divine Truth. She does not think it enough to accept, she dwells upon it; not enough to possess, she uses it; not enough to assent, she develops it; not enough to submit to Reason, she reasons upon it; not indeed reasoning first, and believing afterwards, with Zacharias, yet first believing without reasoning, next from love and reverence, reasoning after believing. And thus she symbolizes to us, not only the faith of the unlearned, but of the doctors of the Church also ...'.[25]

And it seems to me that we can see parallels to this in other attempts to transcend the division introduced into our thought and experience by the Enlightenment. One might think, for instance, of Iris Murdoch's attempt to escape Kant's influence in moral philosophy in her essays in *The Sovereignty of Good.*[26] Kant's separation between reason and the will leads, she argues, to an incredible account of moral activity as centring on moments of conscious moral choice, when in accordance with some moral calculus (which it is the job of moral philosophy to discover) one chooses between this and the other course of action. This tends to suggest that a good man is one who is conscious of the possible courses of action open to him and chooses rightly, whereas, Miss Murdoch suggests, in reality the good man or the saint is not so much conscious of the many possibilities open to him, but rather conscious of only one, the right one, the one demanded by the circumstances. But the notion of moral activity as consisting of a series of moral decisions prepared for by moral reasoning is anyway unrealistic: rather a man acts because he is the sort of person he is, or has become, and 'what we really are seems much more like an

[25] Ibid., pp. 312-13.
[26] London, 1970.

obscure system of energy out of which choices and visible acts of will emerge at intervals in ways which are often unclear and often dependent on the condition of the system in between the moments of choice. If this is so [Miss Murdoch continues] one of the main problems of moral philosophy might be formulated thus: are there any techniques for the purification and reorientation of an energy which is naturally selfish, in such a way that when moments of choice arrive we shall be sure of acting rightly?'[27] Her response to this question is to explore the idea of contemplation, of attention, which releases in the soul 'the capacity to love, that is to *see*' in which 'the liberation of the soul from fantasy consists'.[28] This liberation is the initiation into a freedom which 'is not strictly the exercise of will, but rather the experience of accurate vision which, when this becomes appropriate, occasions action'.[29] To speak in such terms is to revive ideas of a unity in man's soul which transcends any division between reason and the will: 'will and reason then are not entirely separate faculties in the moral agent. Will continually influences belief, for better or worse, and is ideally able to influence it through a sustained attention to reality.'[30] In this holding-together of will and reason, and in her insight into the way in which it is the practice of attention or contemplation, the ability to *see*, that achieves this unity, Iris Murdoch recalls what we have just seen in Newman (and behind both of them—quite consciously and explicitly in Miss Murdoch's case—there is the influence of Greek thought, and especially that of Plato), though she is seeking to revive these ideas in a context that is explicitly atheistic.

Attention, contemplation, *theoria*. For Plato this state, once achieved, was a fundamental, and fundamentally true, relationship to reality, or being. And as Josef Pieper remarks, 'the unique and original relation to being that Plato calls "theoria" can only be realized in its pure state through the sense of wonder, in that purely receptive attitude to reality, undisturbed and

---

[27] Ibid., p. 54.   [28] Ibid., p. 66.
[29] Ibid., p. 67.   [30] Ibid., p. 40.

unsullied by the interjection of the will';[31] and Pieper goes on to underline the place of wonder in philosophy. It is wonder at the mystery of being, at the fact that things are at all: wonder expressed in the age-old cry that Heidegger calls the basic metaphysical question: 'Why, after all, should there be such a thing as being? Why not just nothing?'[32] Such a capacity for wonder can be warped or distorted in various ways. A dulled sensibility will not feel wonder at the mystery of everyday being: it will need the unusual, the sensational, to arouse a sense of wonder. Another distortion of this capacity for wonder, which is the beginning of philosophy, is, Pieper argues, characteristic of modern philosophy. Wonder shakes a man, it disturbs him. And it is this negative, unsettling effect which is all that philosophy since Descartes has noticed. Wonder becomes reduced to doubt, the doubt that threatens a man's intellectual being: if for Socrates wonder was the beginning of philosophy,[33] for Descartes and his followers it is doubt that is the beginning of philosophy. But, asks Pieper, 'does the true sense of wonder really lie in uprooting the mind and plunging it into doubt? Doesn't it really lie in making it possible and indeed necessary to strike yet deeper roots?'[34] Certainly wonder deprives us of what Pieper calls 'penultimate certainties', it is a form of disillusionment. But in all this the positive side is uppermost—the mind is being stripped of illusion and brought face to face with profounder reality: 'the innermost meaning of wonder is fulfilled in a deepened sense of mystery.'[35] But modern philosophy has not seen this, or has evaded it, and instead has concentrated on the phenomenon of doubt, and has sought to overcome it. The Cartesian method is a way of doubt, systematically overcome and made to yield knowledge. Doubt is the beginning of philosophy which ends up as true knowledge when doubt has been left behind. Pieper points out how different this is from the traditional concept of philosophy, which was precisely *philo-sophia*,

---

[31] In his essay 'The Philosophical Act', in *Leisure, the Basis of Culture* (London, 1952), p. 131.

[32] In, e.g., his essay 'Was ist Metaphysik?', reprinted in *Wegmarken* (Frankfurt-am-Main, 2nd edn. 1978), pp. 103-22, referred to by Pieper (n. 31), p. 93.

[33] *Theaetetus*, 155; quoted by Pieper, p. 130.

[34] Pieper, p. 134.

[35] Ibid., p. 135.

the love of wisdom, a love that set out on the quest for wisdom, recognizing that true wisdom is beyond the grasp of the finite creature, man, and is indeed the possession of the gods. Modern philosophy, beginning with doubt, tries to overcome it in seeking a knowledge which it holds to be possible for man (Pieper refers to the preface of Hegel's *Phenomenology of Spirit*); philosophy, in its traditional sense begins in wonder, as man, impelled by his love for wisdom, penetrates more and more deeply into the mystery of reality: 'wonder is not just the starting point of philosophy in the sense of *initium*, of a prelude or preface. Wonder is the *principium*, the lasting source, the *fons et origo,* the immanent origin of philosophy ... The inner form of philosophizing is virtually identical with the inner form of wonder.'[36]

One theme in our considerations that has run through them like a thread has been the notion of *mystery*, and these considerations about the fundamental place of wonder in man's searching after truth return us to this theme. For, to the idea of the permanent place of wonder (in contrast with doubt) corresponds the notion of the essentially irreducible character of mystery. A problem can be solved, a puzzle can be unravelled; but a mystery, if it is truly a mystery, remains. Christians want to speak of the centre of their faith as being the mystery of God in Christ. By that they mean that the problem of existence, the mystery of the ultimate, is truly a mystery: it cannot be unravelled. To say that the problem of existence *is* the mystery of the ultimate is to say that God exists. If the problem of existence can be solved, then there is no need to think of God or bring him into the picture. But to think of God is *not* to solve the problem of existence (as Heidegger thought it did when he maintained that theism was a way of evading the ultimate metaphysical question —Why is there anything and not rather nothing?—by giving a simple 'answer'), but to hold us before the mystery of being. Christians do not simply believe in the mystery of God, but the mystery of God *in* Christ: they believe that in the life and death of a man called Jesus of Nazareth, God lived among us a human life. The mystery of God is not simply the problem of transcendence, nor is it even simply the mystery of immanence—

---

[36] Ibid.

the mystery of intimations of the beyond in the here and now; rather the mystery of God is disclosed in a human life that was lived in history. The life and death and resurrection of Jesus of Nazareth is the place where we meet with the mystery of God. 'Immensity cloister'd in thy dear womb'—the mystery of the ultimate is met with in the particular: not just in the way that the divine is there for us to discern in any particular, but present actively, seeking us out, making itself known to us. Here, more than anywhere else, we realize the true character of mystery: mystery not just as the focus for *our* questioning and investigating, but mystery as that which *questions us*, which calls us to account.

It is the centrality of mystery that is brought into question by any claim by the sciences and the scientific method to total control over the way to truth. Mysteries become problems, problems that are to be solved and can be solved. As we have seen, it is a good scientist who can untangle from the mass of the problematic which confronts him problems that are accessible to the methods he has and will yield to his tools. The penumbra beyond that is ignored for the time being: progress proceeds by the way of the possible. But we have argued that in one crucial point the centrality of mystery is central to the humanities: in that the humanities are concerned with what man has thought and understood and done, and man is a person, and the freedom of the person, the freedom of his will, points to the mystery of man's being. Dissolve that and the humanities fade into the social sciences, and ultimately into 'hard' science. But if we hold to the mystery of the person, then at the heart of the humanities is an engagement between persons—including, indeed especially, the men and women of the past—an engagement in which the mystery of another's personhood calls us into question and challenges our own self-understanding. For mystery does not present itself to us as a datum of which there might be complete, 'objective' knowledge; rather mystery questions us, demands of us a response, challenges us to decide what we are to do, what we are to make of our lives.

If mystery is central to the humanities—and to *human* experience, if it is to remain that—then the importance of theology for the concern of being human is clear: for theology holds before us, and holds us before, the ultimate mystery of God, and suggests that it is because man is made by God in his image and likeness that he is ultimately mysterious and can never be understood as he really is in terms that prescind from the mystery of personhood. Theodor Haecker expressed this well when he affirmed in his 'Dialogue on the Wonderful and on Nothing'[37] that 'to the being of man there belongs also his not-being'.

Consider that I spoke of man who is made not in the image of a machine, but in the image of God, and that he is therefore the most wonderful and the most mysterious among all created beings. How perfectly absurd and meaningless would be the contention: 'to the being of the machine there belongs also its not-being'! For the machine does not belong to these difficult things of which the Preacher speaks, when he says that there will never be an end of what man can say of them. The moment is soon reached, when everything has been said of them. It is not the machine that is wonderful, but man who made it; oh, man is the highest of those things, and in accordance with the statement, 'To the being of man there belongs also his not-being', suffers much to be said about himself, and there will never be an end of it: he is a source of thought which will never be exhausted.[38]

The fundamental thing that Christian theology can contribute, as one way of pursuing knowledge, to all other ways of pursuing knowledge is, as Pieper puts it very well, 'that it should hinder and resist the natural craving of the human spirit for a clear, transparent and definite system'.[39] And it should do this by keeping open access to the tradition which is the vantage-point from which we can behold the mystery of God, which has been revealed in Christ. This does something to explain the peculiar nature of theological discourse, something Newman clearly recognizes in the following passage:

Though the Christian mind reasons out a series of dogmatic statements, one from another, this it has ever done, and always must do, not from those statements taken in themselves, as logical propositions, but as illustrated and (as I may say) inhabited by that sacred impression which is prior to them, which acts as a regulating principle, ever present, upon the reasoning, and without which no one has any warrant to reason at all. Such sentences as 'the Word was God' or 'the Only-begotten Son who is in the bosom of the Father,' or 'the

[37] 'Dialog vom Wunderbaren und vom Nichts', in *Opuscula* (Olten, 1949), pp. 63-91.
[38] Ibid., p. 91.
[39] Pieper (n. 31), p. 160.

Word was made flesh,' or 'the Holy Ghost which proceedeth from the Father,' are not a mere letter which we may handle by the rules of art at our own will, but august tokens of most simple, ineffable, adorable facts, embraced, enshrined, according to its measure, in the believing mind. For though the development of an idea is a deduction of proposition from proposition, these propositions are ever formed in and round the idea itself (so to speak), and are in fact one and all only aspects of it. Moreover, this will account both for the mode of arguing from particular texts or single words of Scripture, practised by the early Fathers, and for their fearless decision in practising it; for the great Object of Faith on which they lived both enabled them to appropriate to itself particular passages of Scripture, and became a safeguard against heretical deductions from them. Also, it will account for the charge of weak reasoning, commonly brought against those Fathers; for never do we seem so illogical to others, as when we are arguing under the continual influence of impressions to which they are insensible.[40]

For theology is not simply a matter of learning, though we risk losing much of the wealth of theological tradition if we despise learning: rather theology is the apprehension of the believing mind combined with a right state of the heart, to use Newman's terms. It is tested and manifest in a life that lives close to the mystery of God in Christ, that preserves for all men a testimony to that mystery which is the object of our faith, and, so far as it is discerned, awakens in the heart a sense of wondering awe which is the light in which we see light.

[40] Newman (n. 10), pp. 335-6.

Index